Harper ▲ ChapelBooks

THE ARCHAEOLOGY

OF THE OLD TESTAMENT

BY R. K. HARRISON

Harper ♦ ChapelBooks

Harper & Row, Publishers, New York

ARCHAEOLOGY OF THE OLD TESTAMENT

THIS BOOK IS DEDICATED IN
AFFECTION AND RESPECT TO
THE RT. REV. ALEXANDER HENRY O'NEIL,
M.A., B.D., D.D., LL.D.,
BISHOP OF FREDERICTON

PREFACE

THIS book is intended to comprise an elementary introduction to the study of Old Testament archaeology for the unprofessional student. It follows the general chronology of the Old Testament so as to relate the Biblical narratives to their contemporary background, and considers only the more significant discoveries in Bible lands. References to source materials have been included in the hope that the work may be of some use to students.

The subject as a whole is important not only for the Old Testament as such but also for the general history of the ancient Near East, in terms of which the culture, history and religion of the Old Testament must be studied. Because the Hebrew were a particular people living in a certain historical period, the significance of the message found in their writings will only be grasped most fully against such a background. For in the last resort, the concern of the Old Testament archaeologist must be a theological one involving the understanding and exposition of the Scriptures. Whilst it must be recognised that archaeological discovery cannot and ought not to be required to prove the "truth" of the Old Testament, it can be expected to furnish such environmental information as will enable us to see the sacred record in true historical and cultural perspective. It is only by this means that we shall begin to appreciate properly the moral and spiritual dimensions of the Divine revelation to man.

I wish to acknowledge my indebtedness for permission to quote from copyright works to the following: to Dr. G. E. Wright for allowing the use of material contained in various numbers of *The Biblical Archaeologist*; to the University of Chicago Press for permission to reprint sections from A. Heidel, *The Gilgamesh Epic and Old Testament Parallels* (1949 edition), A. Heidel, *The Babylonian Genesis* (1951 edition), and D. D. Luckenbill, *Ancient Records of Assyria and Babylonia* (2 volumes, 1926); to the American Philosophical Society for their kindness in allowing the use of copyright material in S. N. Kramer, *Sumerian Mythology* (1947 edition), originally published in 1944 in Volume 21 of the Society's *Memoirs*, and to Dr. Kramer himself for his gracious consent; to Princeton University Press for permitting quotations from J. Finegan, *Light From the Ancient Past* (1946) and J. B. Pritchard (Ed.), *Ancient Near Eastern Texts Relating to the Old Testament* (1950); and to the Clarendon Press of Oxford for allowing the use of material in S. L. Caiger, *Bible and Spade* (1936) and R. H. Charles (Ed.), *The Apocrypha and Pseudepigrapha of the Old Testament* (2 volumes, 1913).

In the preparation of this work I was encouraged by the kindly interest and help of a former colleague, the Rev. Dr. A. H. Crowfoot, a relative of the eminent archaeologist. My thanks are also due to Mrs. H. Bohne, Assistant Librarian of Wycliffe College, Toronto, for her patient help with source materials. Finally I am particularly grateful to my colleague, the Rev. Norman Green, Field Secretary of Wycliffe College, for his expert assistance with the photographic section of this book.

Wycliffe College,   R. K. Harrison
University of Toronto

CONTENTS

PLATES

ABBREVIATIONS

1QS	*The Community Rule* or *Manual of Discipline.*
CDC	*Cairo Damascene Covenanters.*
1QISa	St. Mark's Monastery Isaiah Scroll.
1QISb	Hebrew University's Isaiah Scroll.
1QpHab	The Qumran Habakkuk Commentary.
A.V.	The Authorised (King James) Version (1611).
R.V.	The Revised Version (1881).
R.S.V.	The Revised Standard Version (1952).
AASOR	*The Annual of the American Schools of Oriental Research.*
AB	G. A. Barton, *Archaeology and the Bible* (1946 edition).
ADSS	J. M. Allegro, *The Dead Sea Scrolls* (1956).
AJA	*American Journal of Archaeology.*
ANE	J. B. Pritchard (Ed.), *The Ancient Near East* (1958).
ANET	J. B. Pritchard (Ed.), *Ancient Near Eastern Texts Relating to the Old Testament* (1950).
AP	W. F. Albright, *The Archaeology of Palestine* (1949).
APOT	R. H. Charles (Ed.), *The Apocrypha and Pseudepigrapha of the Old Testament* (1913). 2 vols.
ARAB	D. D. Luckenbill, *Ancient Records of Assyria and Babylonia* (1926). 2 vols.
ARE	J. H. Breasted, *Ancient Records of Egypt* (1906-7). 5 vols.
ARI	W. F. Albright, *Archaeology and the Religion of Israel* (1955).

BA   *The Biblical Archaeologist.*

BASOR   *Bulletin of the American Schools of Oriental Research.*

BCNE   H. Frankfort, *The Birth of Civilisation in the Near East* (1956).

BDSS   M. Burrows, *The Dead Sea Scrolls* (1955).

BG   A. Heidel, *The Babylonian Genesis* (1951 edition).

BHI   J. Bright, *A History of Israel* (1960).

BJRL   *Bulletin of the John Rylands Library.*

CAEM   A. L. Perkins, *The Comparative Archaeology of Early Mesopotamia* (1949).

CBQ   *Catholic Biblical Quarterly.*

CCK   D. J. Wiseman, *Chronicles of Chaldean Kings (626-556 B.C.) in the British Museum* (1956).

DJD   D. Barthélemy and J. T. Milik, *Discoveries in the Judean Desert* I. Qumran, Cave I (1955); II Murabba'at (1961).

DOTT   D. Winton Thomas (Ed.) *Documents from Old Testament Times* (1958).

DSSHU   E. L. Sukenik (Ed.) *The Dead Sea Scrolls of the Hebrew University* (1955).

FSAC   W. F. Albright, *From the Stone Age to Christianity* (1957 edition).

IOTT   C. H. Gordon, *Introduction to Old Testament Times* (1953).

JBL   *Journal of Biblical Literature*

JEA   *Journal of Egyptian Archaeology.*

JNES   *Journal of Near Eastern Studies.*

JQR   *Jewish Quarterly Review.* New Series.

JRAS   *The Journal of the Royal Asiatic Society.*

LAP   J. Finegan, *Light From the Ancient Past* (1946).

NLMAE   V. G. Childe, *New Light From the Most Ancient East* (1953 edition).

OTC   H. C. Alleman and E. E. Flack (Ed.) *Old Testament Commentary* (1954).

PEQ   *Palestine Exploration Quarterly.*

PJB	*Palästinajahrbuch.*
RB	*Revue Biblique.*
TH	O. R. Gurney, *The Hittites* (1952).
TJ	L. Finkelstein (Ed.) *The Jews; Their History, Culture and Religion* (1949). 2 vols.
TS	C. L. Woolley, *The Sumerians* (1928).
UC	C. L. Woolley, *Ur of the Chaldees* (1950 edition).
UL	C. H. Gordon, *Ugaritic Literature* (1949).
VDJD	G. Vermès, *Discovery in the Judean Desert* (1956).
VT	*Vetus Testamentum.*
WBA	G. E. Wright, *Biblical Archaeology* (1957).
WHAB	G. E. Wright and F. V. Filson, *Westminster Historical Atlas to the Bible* (1953).
WMTS	M. Burrows, *What Mean These Stones?* (1941).
ZAW	*Zeitschrift für die alttestamentliche Wissenschaft.*
ZFDSS	H. H. Rowley, *The Zadokite Fragments and the Dead Sea Scrolls* (1952).

Chapter I

MESOPOTAMIAN ORIGINS

SCATTERED throughout the Near East are many curious earthen formations in the general shape of a rounded hill or a truncated cone. Differing considerably in size and distribution, they may rise from the emptiness of an undulating plain or may occupy a strategic position on a rocky plateau overlooking a mountain pass. Such structures are described by the word *tell*,[1] a Semitic term used of a mound containing the remains of long-ruined cities. The location of the *tell* was generally such as to make it desirable for the city to be rebuilt on the same site when necessary, a process which was occasionally repeated as often as eight or nine times. The successive occupational levels thus furnished the history of the immediate area, the lowest deposits being the most ancient.[2] When confronted with such a site the first responsibility of the archaeologist is to excavate it meticulously and preserve or restore such artefacts as he may encounter. He must then evaluate this material historically on the basis of stratigraphic (the assembly of artefacts recovered from the various levels), typological (the classification and historical study of the objects) and ceramic (pottery) examination. Seismic activity at an earlier period frequently complicates the situation, whilst other difficulties[3] often limit the degree of success experienced in relating the discoveries to ancient Near Eastern history and culture.

Many early mounds occur in Mesopotamia, the land of the Tigris and Euphrates. These two great rivers were indispensable to the fertility of the Babylonian plain, which when developed by means of irrigation canals[4] saw a great increase in population. Some of the earliest inhabited sites belong to the Neolithic period (*c.* 6000-4500 B.C.) of northern Mesopotamia. A number of village settlements located in the same general area include the mound at Nineveh, the *tell* at Tepe Gawra some twelve miles to the north-east, and Tell Hassuna south of modern Mosul, all of which are good representatives of the period. At Tell Hassuna the most primitive settlers possessed coarse pottery and obsidian tools, while their successors used rather more elaborate ceramic ware[5] and lived in rude huts. In 1931 Professor M. E. L. Mallowan took soundings of the mound at Nineveh to a depth of ninety feet,[6] and uncovered the remains of prehistoric villages beneath the lowest strata of Assyrian culture. Decayed wood and ashes were all that remained of the huts which had first been built on the site, while the pottery, which consisted of coarse dishes, was marked by notches and other crude attempts at decoration. The earliest levels of the mound at Tepe Gawra contained a number of Neolithic skeletons beside which were buried several kinds of plain and decorated pottery, some of delicate texture.[7] All these primitive communities seem to have grown up side by side for economic reasons, and their stage of cultural development indicates that the Mesopotamians of the New Stone Age were far from uncivilised.[8]

Their successors in the Chalcolithic or "copper-stone" period (*c.* 4500-3000 B.C.) introduced the true culture of antiquity into northern Mesopotamia. The first traces of this period were unearthed at Tell Halaf by Baron von Oppenheim just prior to the First World War[9] and are known as Halafian. This designation accords with the general practice of classifying the different cultural stages in terms of the sites where they were first discovered. The lowest levels exhibited definite advances upon the Neolithic period as indicated by the houses, which were generally erected upon a stone foundation and grouped around a central shrine. In its earliest form the latter consisted of a single circular room, but later structures had an additional anteroom somewhat similar to the pre-pottery Neolithic shrines of Jericho. Rough figurines of domesticated animals were recovered at Tell Halaf, as well as some representations of the human torso bearing exaggerated sexual features reminiscent of earlier Aurignacian practice.[10] Weaving was a well-established craft by this time, and the secret of copper-smelting had also been discovered.

But the most important feature of Halafian culture was the painted pottery which was unearthed from the lowest levels. It was thin, hand-made, and fired in closed kilns which afforded excellent temperature control.[11] By this means a delicate glazed and decorated ceramic ware was produced, exhibiting patterns and designs of a geometrical nature which were occasionally replaced by rough outlines of animals and human beings. One Halafian vase was decorated with the picture of a wheeled vehicle, perhaps a chariot, carrying a man. It represents the earliest drawing of a spoked wheel, and testifies to the great antiquity of chariots and similar conveyances. Most archaeologists agree that the design, texture and manufacture of Halafian pottery was unsurpassed in antiquity.[12] Halafian deposits have also been found at Tell Arpachiyah near Nineveh, at Carchemish, and elsewhere.

The extensive swamps of the lower Tigris-Euphrates region impeded the cultural development of southern Mesopotamia, and it was only when some of these areas were drained and irrigated that prehistoric villages could flourish. The oldest settlement in Babylonia was unearthed at Tell el-Obeid, a low mound four miles north-west of Ur.[13] Woolley and Hall dated the earliest levels at about 4000 B.C.,[14] and from them they removed the remains of houses, pottery, flint implements and weapons. Since stone was non-existent in the area the dwellings were made of reeds plastered with mud. At a later period sun-dried mud bricks were used, and the buildings were waterproofed by the addition of decorative clay mosaics to the walls, a device which was to persist for some centuries.[15] The pottery was finely textured, and the palish green colour was relieved by means of brown or black geometrical designs.

This general period saw the erection of more substantial buildings in Assyria, and a late Obeid stratum (XIII) at Tepe Gawra,[16] dated at the end of the fifth millennium B.C., revealed the existence of three large shrines surrounding a main courtyard. The construction of the temples was characterised by a series of niches recessed vertically into the walls, a feature which dominated Mesopotamian temple architecture for many centuries.[17] Obeid deposits have also been reported from Erech, Ur, Eridu and Uruk.

The next cultural phase, generally known as the Uruk period, is probably dated towards the end of the fourth millennium B.C. The site of ancient Uruk, the Erech of Genesis 10:10, was excavated by Jordan,[18] who found black, grey and red ceramic ware which had been fashioned on a potter's wheel. He also uncovered traces of the first Babylonian *ziggurat*[19] which was approximately forty-five yards square. The shrine erected on the mound was about sixty-five feet in length and fifty feet in width. Its outer walls exhibited the characteristic vertical recesses, and some of the original decorative whitewash still clung to the mud bricks. Another building was patterned with mosaics of clay cones executed in three colours and reminiscent of Obeid patterns.[20]

The first known use of the cylinder seal was found at Uruk. The Obeid period had produced a decorative button-like stamp which was employed to identify property.[21] In late Uruk times it was replaced by the stone cylinder seal[22] on which was engraved a design or picture in relief. When rolled on a soft clay tablet it left a distinctive impression which in later times claimed considerable artistic merit. Another notable achievement of this culture was the emergence of a rough pictographic script on clay tablets. It was the precursor of Babylonian cuneiform, and in appearance constituted a crude representation of the object involved. As speed and ability in writing increased it was gradually reduced to a system of corresponding line groups. When the triangular stylus came into vogue the pictographs assumed the characteristic wedge-shaped cuneiform writing. The texts of Uruk tablets were written in perpendicular columns from left to right, and employed a sexagesimal system of computation common at a later stage.[23]

Excavations at Jemdet Nasr[24] in northern Mesopotamia revealed the increasing complexity of civilised life at the beginning of the third millennium B.C. Pictographic writing was at a more advanced stage than at Uruk, and bronze came into use for the first time in Mesopotamia. The scope of agriculture was widened with the cultivation of wheat, barley, grapes, figs, olives, onions, beans and other vegetables,[25] while in the realm of art the Jemdet Nasr period produced the first evidence of sculpture in stone. Contemporary levels at Ur and Uruk displayed similar artistic achievements in basalt and soapstone media. The typical ceramic ware is generally held to be inferior to earlier Chalcolithic pottery, being characterised by yellow or black patterns on a red background. During this period the ancient cities of Eshnunna, Kish and Shuruppak were established, and it is from these sites that much of the information concerning the late Chalcolithic period of Mesopotamia has been derived.

The proto-literate phase of southern Mesopotamia was marked by systematic attempts to drain the rich alluvial mud deposited from the upper reaches of the Tigris and Euphrates, to establish some measure of flood control, and to develop the enormous agricultural potential of the area.[26] So successful were the efforts expended in this direction that by the end of the fourth millennium B.C. the inhabitants to the south were cultivating as wide a range of cereal and vegetable crops as the people in northern Mesopotamia.

With the expansion of agriculture the small villages of the Obeid phase grew into a number of city-states which controlled adjacent territory. Each claimed a patron deity who was regarded as the real owner of the land. Throughout ancient Mesopotamia the sacred shrine was accorded the central position in the community, and the priesthood took a leading part in the organisation and development of the local economy. The chief priest or *patesi* became known as the *ishakku* or "tenant-farmer" in deference to the concept of the divine ownership of the land. In effect the *patesi* was a civil governor who organised priests and people alike so as to bring communal life to the highest possible level of development.[27]

Some authorities have maintained that this centralising of organisational effort provided the stimulus for the invention of writing.[28] At Uruk the earliest tablets found in the Red Temple were memoranda connected with community activities. Inscribed in a rough pictographic script, they included lists of animals involved in business transactions, numerical records attested by means of cylinder-seal impressions, and wage-lists with entries accompanied by the comment, "beer and bread for one day". From the available evidence it would appear that all members of the community were of equal social status, and were held responsible for the productivity of their land-allotments.[29]

About 4000 B.C. a people of superior intellectual calibre entered the marshy delta region of southern Mesopotamia. Known as the Sumerians, after the name of their capital Sumer, they were a swarthy, non-Semitic people who attained cultural dominance from an early period. They may have come either from the Caucasus or from the mountains to the east, and were associated with another non-Semitic group, the Elamites, with whom they came into frequent conflict. The Sumerians, or "black-headed people" as they called themselves, enlarged the Obeid

system of city-states. They were highly religious, and set
about developing theological concepts which exercised an
enormous influence in the Near East for many centuries.
A list of deities was drawn up, prominent amongst whom
were Anu and Enlil, and theocratic rule began to assume a
new prominence. Temples were enlarged, and the energetic
Sumerians laboured to increased the productivity of the
land.

From the nature of the articles contained in the temple
store-rooms[30] it would appear that craftsmen were active
at this period. A trading-route extending from northern
India to Egypt passed through Sumerian territory, and
the wealth of the alluvial plain resulted in increased trade
with the surrounding peoples. Even in the Jemdet Nasr
phase semi-precious stones such as obsidian and lapis
lazuli had been imported into Mesopotamia, and with the
expansion of the Sumerian economy there came a significant
increase in commercial dealings with India, Asia Minor and
Syria. Craftsmen fashioned large quantities of toilet sets,
gold and silver pins, brooches, clasps and ear-rings. New
types of agricultural implements such as ploughs were
invented and ultimately exported to neighbouring countries.
The decorated pottery of earlier phases was replaced to
a large extent by vessels magnificently executed in gold,
silver and bronze. An extremely high degree of cultural
development is indicated by the artistic skill necessary for
such superb productions.

As the community enlarged in the early dynastic period
the authority vested in the temple priests was gradually
concentrated in the personage of a ruler or *lugal*.[31] Originally
such kingship was temporary, since the *lugal* was at best
only a deputy of the deity which patronised the city-state.[32]
An executive temple priest, the *ensi*, organised the whole of
communal life and in time of war was responsible for
mobilising the people and controlling military forces.
Somewhat after 3000 B.C. the office of *lugal* became heredi-

tary and dynasties resulted. In the religious language of
later times, Sumerian kingship was "lowered from on
high" and established first in Eridu. An ancient Sumerian
king-list, probably compiled during the Third Dynasty of
Ur, was published by Professor Langdon in 1923.[33] Known
as the Weld-Blundell prism, it contained the names of
the kings who reigned before a disastrous flood interrupted
Sumerian affairs. The eight rulers mentioned were credited
with reigns of exaggerated length in Eridu, Badtibira,
Larak, Sippar and Shuruppak.[34]

Mesopotamia had been subject to sudden inundations
from time immemorial, and the tradition of a great flood or
series of floods was firmly established in the early dynastic
period of Sumeria. Several literary versions of this event
were compiled, some of which spoke of Shuruppak as the
site of the deluge. A fragmentary Sumerian tablet recovered
from Nippur and dated in the third millennium B.C. has
preserved a dramatic account of this memorable incident.
It was inscribed on both sides and contained six columns
in all. The first of these spoke of creation:

> "After Anu, Enlil, Enki and Ninhursag had created the
> dark headed peoples . . . the cattle of the field . . . on
> the plains he called them into being . . ."[35]

Regretting their creative activity the gods determined
to destroy mankind, and the third column spoke of the
distress of Ishtar (Ninhursag) and of Ziusudra, the pious
king-priest who was the Sumerian counterpart of Noah, at
this decision. The fourth column contained a revelation to
Ziusudra from Enka, the powerful water-god, advising
him of the plan:

> "Ziusudra, standing . . . heard (a voice) . . . 'I will speak
> a word to thee . . . By our hand a rainflood . . . will be
> (sent); to destroy the seed of mankind . . .' ".[36]

The fifth column described the way in which Ziusudra survived the tremendous deluge:

> "All the windstorms, exceedingly powerful, attacked as
> one . . .
> After, for seven days and seven nights,
> The deluge had raged in the land,
> And the huge boat had been tossed about on the great
> waters . . .
> Ziusudra opened *a window* of the huge boat . . .
> Before Utu[37] prostrated himself.
> The king kills an ox, slaughters a sheep."[38]

At the end of the ordeal the king-priest became immortal and was translated to the "mountain of Dilmun".[39]

Excavations at Shuruppak in the late Jemdet Nasr levels[40] revealed the presence of a large alluvial deposit, while at Kish a somewhat similar flood stratum measured eighteen inches in depth.[41] Langdon[42] described the latter in terms of the Noachian flood, and an eight-foot alluvial deposit at Ur, dating from the middle Obeid period, was similarly interpreted by Woolley.[43] This attempt at correlation illustrates some of the difficulties which beset the interpretation of archaeological material. In the first instance the alluvial levels at Ur and Kish are not contemporary. Similar deposits at Shuruppak, Kish, Uruk and Lagash do not correspond with the dating of the Ur stratum.[44] Furthermore the excavations of Watelin at Kish uncovered several such alluvial layers, two of the more significant being separated by a nineteen-foot section of debris. At Tell el-Obeid, some four miles from Ur, there were no traces of water-laid strata when Woolley excavated the site.[45]

It is clearly difficult to associate any one of these deposits with the Flood of Genesis, since positive identification is not merely lacking but is highly improbable.[46] Indeed there are some who maintain that Mesopotamian archaeology has revealed no trace of the Noachian flood whatever.[47] Nevertheless it is a fact that sedimentary levels occurring at different periods can be demonstrated at numerous Mesopotamian sites. These deposits may have resulted from torrential rains or perhaps from a tidal wave.[48] There can be no doubt that periodic inundations were a dreaded feature of life in Babylonia, and it is probable that one such cataclysm was commemorated in religious literature. Since the excavations have shown that not all cities were equally inundated, the Noachian deluge was evidently comparatively localised, and of importance for later Semitic tradition because it had a moral basis, unlike other floods, and involved the ancestors of the Biblical Patriarchs.

When Kish was excavated Watelin discovered cylinder impressions of Gilgamesh, the legendary hero of Babylonian epic poetry, at levels beneath the one identified by Langdon with the Genesis flood.[49] This indicated that the Babylonian deluge story was already known at Kish, which would make it a very ancient religious tradition indeed. In the nature of the case it is impossible to state with certainty the origin either of the Babylonian or Hebrew accounts of the Flood. The most that can be said for the latter is that it commemorates an event which left a lasting impression upon the Hebrew mind, and which cannot at present be related to one specific archaeological level.

Similar problems of recovery and identification are connected with Noah's Ark. Accounts of the dimensions of this vessel present certain difficulties,[50] but it would appear that a structure of unusual proportions was involved. The mountains of Ararat (Genesis 8:4), the traditional resting-place of the Ark, may be identified with the *Urartu* of Assyrian inscriptions which corresponds to the modern Armenia, though this is by no means certain. From time to time attempts have been made to recover pieces of the "original ark",[51] and carbon-14 dating[52] of wooden fragments from northern Mesopotamia has corroborated the antiquity of the material under examination. But to presume to identify specimens of this kind with Noah's Ark is both unscientific and illogical. In the first instance it is highly unlikely that the Ark could have survived to the present day in any form. Secondly, even if remains of an ancient vessel were recovered from a probable site, it would be almost impossible to state with certainty that they were part of Noah's Ark.

After the great deluge kingship was again "lowered from heaven", being resumed according to the Sumerian king-list[53] with the first dynasty of Kish. Contemporary dynasties appear to have been established at Uruk, Mari, Ur and elsewhere. At Ur the early dynastic period culminated in the rise of the First Dynasty, during which four kings reigned for a total of one hundred and seventy seven years, according to the king-list. This inscription claimed that Mes-Anne-pada was the founder of the First Dynasty, and this was dramatically confirmed by the discovery of a tablet at Tell el-Obeid dated *c.* 2700 B.C. which read, "A Anne-pada king of Ur, son of Mes-Anne-pada, king of Ur, has built this for his Lady Ninkharsag".[54]

The excavations of Woolley at Ur have demonstrated graphically the advanced degree of culture attained during the First Dynasty. Decorated columns and mosaic work depicting rural scenes were elaborately executed in temples and other buildings, as were several copper bulls which were recovered in fragmentary condition from the same levels.[55] In a burial area outside the walls of the primitive city Woolley found the decayed remains of wickerwork and wooden coffins along with funerary objects such as cups, vessels, weapons, tools and jewelry. At a lower level he made the startling discovery of the celebrated "royal tombs" of Ur.[56] That they were the graves of important personages was apparent immediately, since they were constructed principally from limestone blocks which must have been brought from a considerable distance. One tomb had been placed on top of the other, and the excavators found that the lower vault had been plundered. Still remaining, however, were a silver model of a boat and a cylinder seal containing the name of the deceased person, A-bar-gi. The occupant of the upper chamber had been placed upon a wooden bier, and was identified from a lapis lazuli cylinder as Lady Shub-ad. A gold cup lay near her hand and her headdress, richly fashioned from gold and silver and adorned with semi-precious stones, was still in good condition.[57]

A burial pit adjacent to the tomb of A-bar-gi revealed the remains of more than sixty persons, while a comparable one for the Lady Shub-ad contained the bones of about twenty-five people. The two principal personages were apparently husband and wife, and Woolley concluded that their deaths had been marked by a form of voluntary sacrifice employed only to honour deceased royal persons.[58] There were no obvious signs of violence on the bodies of the attendants, which were laid out in an orderly fashion and accompanied by jewelry, weapons, vessels and the like. Other death pits contained the remains of horses and chariots as well as various funerary objects. Amongst the latter were some beautifully inlaid harps and two statues of goats standing erect before a bush.[59] The general standard of workmanship is extremely high, and can best be illustrated by the magnificent golden helmet recovered from the grave of "Mes-kalam-dug, Hero of the Good Land". It was fashioned from solid gold in the form of a wig, with the locks of hair hammered in relief and the individual hairs engraved in delicate symmetrical lines.[60]

The largest of the stone vaults yielded the so-called "Standard of Ur", whose superb execution in mosaic work spoke eloquently of the artistic achievements in the First Dynasty. It consisted of a wooden panel twenty-two inches long and nine inches wide, with triangular end-pieces. From its portrayal of Sumerian military equipment[61] has arisen the suggestion that it was carried in processions as a banner or standard. When restored the mosaic work filled both sides of the panel and depicted the themes of War and Peace by means of three rows of shell figures set in a background of lapis lazuli. The War theme showed fully-armed infantry wearing heavy clothing and drawn up in close order. They carried axes and wore copper helmets, as distinct from the lightly-armed infantry preceding them who carried axes, daggers and short swords. Several four-wheeled chariots drawn by four asses and containing a warrior armed with a javelin completed the military array. The Peace panel depicted a sumptuous royal banquet at which musicians entertained the king and his guests. This remarkable artefact is another eloquent witness to the advanced level of cultural attainment which characterised the First Dynasty of Ur.

About this time Eannatum, ruler of Lagash, began to make war on the more southerly cities of Ur, Kish and Uruk. A successor, Urukagina, was a notable humanitarian who instituted administrative reforms to check priestly corruption and enforce observance of the "righteous laws" of the god Ningirsu.[62] Many years later Hammurabi drew upon this legal material in formulating his celebrated code of laws.

During the middle of the fourth millennium B.C. some semi-nomadic Semitic tribes settled in the northern areas of the plain of Shinar and established trade with Sumeria at the beginning of the third millennium. About 2400 B.C. they rose to power under Sargon, who as an infant had been placed in a reed ark and set adrift on the river Euphrates. He established the city of Agade, from which his people received the designation of Akkadians, and about 2355 B.C. he defeated the powerful Lugalzagesi of Sumeria, conquered the entire Babylonian plain and established a Semitic empire. Sargon assimilated the bulk of Sumerian

cultural achievements into his dynasty, but replaced the
native tongue with his own Semitic dialect, thus making
Sumerian a classical language. Trade and commerce
flourished at this time, and excavations at Gasur (Yorgan
Tepe) have shown the extent of contemporary business
activity. One tablet, apparently a sketch to show the position
of an estate, is probably the oldest map known to man.
Buying and selling on the instalment system were also
prominent in this period.[63] A revolution in artistic standards
brought Akkadian art to new levels of execution, as illustrated by the Victory Stele of Naram-Sin, grandson of
Sargon.[64]

Nippur, Lagash and Shuruppak were strongholds of an
extensive mythology in the third millennium B.C. This
material drew heavily upon the earliest Sumerian accounts
of the deities and their activities, but was rewritten and
modified by the Akkadian scribes to the point where the
resulting liturgical myths and epic poems were much
superior to their Sumerian precursors. These compositions
were generally held to furnish a definitive statement of
Akkadian religious tenets, and so conservative were the
Babylonians in matters of religion that the lists of deities
drawn up in the second millennium B.C. and found on
tablets recovered from Shuruppak and Lagash were regarded
as canonical throughout the entire period of Babylonian
history.[65]

Naram-Sin's great empire fell to the Gutians, a Caucasian
people, in the reign of his son Shargalisharri (*c.* 2180 B.C.),
and Babylonia declined in influence. A century later a
remarkable ruler named Gudea governed Lagash and
ushered in a dramatic revival of Sumerian culture. This
was the magnificent Third Dynasty of Ur (*c.* 2070-1960
B.C.), whose first ruler was Ur-Nammu, "King of Sumer
and Akkad". He erected a massive *ziggurat* at Ur, which
was excavated by Woolley in 1922.[66] The tower originally
stood about seventy feet high, whilst its base was two

hundred feet long and one hundred and fifty feet wide. The centre consisted of unbaked mud brick, and was faced to a depth of eight feet with a veneer of baked brick set in bitumen. The design was unique in that there were no straight lines in the building. Instead, carefully calculated slopes and curves achieved an optical illusion of lightness and strength which was to be popular centuries later with the Greek builders of the Athenian Parthenon.[67] The uppermost stage housed the shrine of the Moon deity Nannar, and provided a fitting crown for the entire structure.

A fragmentary *stele* of Ur-Nammu recovered from the site depicted various stages in the construction of the *ziggurat*. The king was represented as a workman carrying compasses, a pick and a trowel,[68] while one of the panels exhibited a flying angel pouring out lifegiving water upon the earth.[69] The business area connected with the temple showed that factories and workshops had been expanded to meet the needs of an increasing populace, one such structure producing twelve varieties of woollen cloth. Several tablets found in the ruins gave the names of the weavers, their rations of food, the amount of wool issued to them, and the quantity of the material which they wove.[70] Business records also recovered from the site were found to consist of ledgers and accounts.

About 1960 B.C. the prosperous Third Dynasty was threatened by Amorite raids from the north, and at the same time the Elamites swept down from the hills to the east and sacked Ur. A tablet found at Nippur described the destruction:

"The sacred dynasty from the temple they exiled,
They demolished the city, they demolished the temple,
They seized the rulership of the land . . ."[71]

The once-united empire of Akkad and Sumer resorted

to the old concept of city-states, and it was not until the following century that an obscure Amorite gained control of a small city named Bab-ilu or Babylon, and established the First Babylonian Dynasty (*c.* 1830 B.C.). For a time its very existence was threatened by the more powerful cities to the south, but under Hammurabi (*c.* 1704-1662 B.C.) it became the dominant political force in Babylonia.

This man was an outstanding military and political figure who brought great organising ability to bear upon his kingdom. Although little has survived of Babylon as it was in his day,[72] sufficient has been discovered to indicate the earliest attempts at town-planning, with streets intersecting at right angles and property arranged systematically in blocks. His most notable achievement, however, was his celebrated legal code. In the days of Ur-Nammu and Dungi civil law had consisted of oral decisions rendered largely on an *ad hoc* basis. Hammurabi collected several of these Sumerian legal codes and modified them to suit the needs of contemporary society.

J. de Morgan unearthed a copy of the resulting legislation in 1901 at Susa, where it had been carried by marauding Elamites about 1200 B.C. It consisted of a black diorite *stele* about six feet in height[73] depicting Hammurabi standing before Shamash, the sun-deity and patron of justice. Fifty one columns of cuneiform commenced with a prologue which stated that Hammurabi had been commanded by the gods to "make righteousness shine forth in the land, to destroy the wrongdoer and the wicked man . . . and to illumine the land."

The laws themselves consisted of nearly three hundred sections[74] and were promulgated in the second year of his reign.[75] They dealt with a wide variety of social, commercial, domestic and moral issues, and were of particular importance because they constituted the first major attempt to establish society upon a rational, non-magical basis. Violations of morality were viewed in a serious light, and the penalty prescribed for adultery was death. A marriage was only recognised by the law when recorded in writing, and both parties had the right of divorce. Society was divided into three classes consisting of the *awilum* or patrician, the *mushkenum* or free artisan, and the *wardum* or chattel-slave. When wrong or injury required legal satisfaction the principle of *lex talionis* or retaliation in kind was applied to accommodate the various levels of society. Medical fees were governed by a similar procedure, and malpractice was discouraged by stern legislation. The building of houses, rental of cattle, tax-collection, river navigation, wages and many other matters were dealt with in the Code, reflecting a highly complex background of political and social life.

Parallels have frequently been drawn between the Code of Hammurabi and the Mosaic legislation.[76] That similarities should exist is hardly surprising in view of the closeness of racial antecedence and cultural outlook. In the matter of adultery the Code (section 129) and the Mosaic Law (Leviticus 20:10; Deuteronomy 22:22) prescribed the death penalty for both offenders. In Exodus 21:16, as in the Code of Hammurabi (section 14), the kidnapping and selling of a person was a capital offence. The principle of retaliation enunciated in Exodus 21:23ff., and Deuteronomy 19:21 is identical with that underlying many sections of the Hammurabi legislation (*e.g.* sections 197, 210, 230). Of some significance is the fact that the Mosaic code diverged from that of Hammurabi (section 142) in refusing women equal rights of divorce. Ethical and spiritual principles were not conspicuous in the laws of Hammurabi, and in general his code placed an inferior valuation upon human life as compared with the enactments of Moses.

The stability which Hammurabi brought to Babylonia encouraged the priestly classes to pursue a variety of literary and educational interests. A remarkable degree of proficiency was attained in medicine, botany and geology,[77] whilst

mathematical and astronomical texts indicated an acquain-
tance with a wide range of mathematical problems.[78] Religious
traditions were modified to give pride of place to Marduk,
patron deity of Babylon, whose exploits were commemorated
in a lengthy creation epic. Sometimes known as *enuma elish*
from its opening words, this composition was first discovered in the ruined library of Ashurbanipal (668-626
B.C.) at Nineveh. Other fragments have been recovered
from Ashur, Uruk and Kish, and are relatively late in date.

Whilst the epic depended upon Sumerian originals, its
present form originated in the time of Hammurabi. It
consisted of about one thousand lines written on seven
tablets linked in series, and began with a mention of the
two mythical divine personages of Sumerian tradition,
Apsu the underground sweet-water reservoir and Tiamat
the salt-water ocean,[79] whose boisterous offspring very
nearly brought about their own destruction. They were
championed by Marduk who slew Tiamat in battle,[80]
established the earth and organised the celestial constellations:

"The moon he caused to shine forth; the night he
  entrusted (to her).
He appointed her . . . to make known the days.
Monthly without ceasing to go forth with a tiara . . ."[81]

The sixth tablet described the creation of humanity from
the blood of Kingu, an ally of Tiamat. Following Sumerian
tradition man was considered vastly inferior to the deities,
amounting almost to a divine afterthought. The concluding
tablet described the elevation of Marduk to the leadership
of the entire Babylonian pantheon.

There are similarities between this epic and the creation
narratives in Genesis. Both begin with a watery chaos and
end with the Creator in repose, whilst the sequence of
creative events follows the same general order. However,
it is a scientific axiom that in all questions of comparison

PLATE 2. *Semites in Egypt.*
Trading Asiatics such as these depicted from the late Middle Kingdom period were frequent visitors to Egypt.

PLATE 1. *Mesopotamian cylinder seals.*
The impressions, produced in relief on moist clay, show various mythological creatures and deities.

PLATE 3. *The Rosetta Stone.*
Discovered in 1799 by Napoleon's engineers in Egypt, the trilingual
inscription in old hieroglyphic, demotic Egyptian and Greek, led to
the decipherment of ancient Egyptian.

differences are much more significant than similarities, and whilst certain common sources may underly both narratives,[82] the finished products exhibit dramatic divergences in content, style and spiritual value, making the Genesis accounts far superior in nature.

Another celebrated composition emerging from the First Babylonian Dynasty was the Epic of Gilgamesh,[83] also recovered from Nineveh. It described the adventures of the legendary Sumerian ruler of Uruk at the end of the fourth millennium B.C., who on the death of his friend Enkidu went to look for the plant of life. The eleventh tablet is of interest because it preserved the Babylonian account of the Deluge. In this version Utnapishtim, keeper of the healing plant, told Gilgamesh that the gods were planning to devastate Shuruppak by means of a flood. Utnapishtim was ordered to build an ark, and shortly after it was completed a terrible storm arose which flooded the land:

> "Six days and (six) nights
> the wind blew, the downpour, the tempest (and) the
>   flood
> When the seventh day arrived . . .
> The sea grew quiet, the storm abated, the flood
>   ceased.
> I opened a window and light fell upon my face . . .
> On Mount Nisir the ship landed . . ."[84]

The name Utnapishtim ("Day of Life") is the Semitic Babylonian form of the Sumerian Ziusudra. Other features of the Epic point to dependence upon Sumerian liturgical sources.

In the second half of the third millennium B.C. a people known as the Hurrians swept down into Mesopotamia from the mountains to the north-east. Familiar to the Biblical authors as Horites[85] they became an important ethnic group in the Near East. While traces of their culture have been found near Amorite sites in Syria and Palestine, their chief centre was Nuzu, some one hundred miles southeast of Nineveh. Archaeological excavations at this site[86] have uncovered thousands of tablets dated in the fifteenth century B.C. and written in Babylonian cuneiform with the addition of a few native Hurrian loan-words. The tablets contained many kinds of detailed records, showing that Hurrian customs and laws were in striking accord with those current amongst the Hebrew Patriarchs as reflected in the records of the Book of Genesis.

In the days of Rim-Sin of Larsa, an older contemporary of Hammurabi, there arose in Mesopotamia a group of people known from inscriptions and tablets as Habiru,[87] who at other times were often designated by the ideogram SA.GAZ. Of obscure origin they appeared in a variety of roles including raiders, mercenary soldiers, captives, musicians, domestic servants, government employees and landless soldiers. Albright has maintained that their designation was more properly ᶜApiru,[88] a form closely related to ᶜIbhri, the Biblical Hebrews. Whilst there are certain unsolved philological problems connected with this matter, it may well be that the Hebrews were a small group within the larger Habiru society. Certainly it would not be out of harmony with Hebrew tradition to associate their origins with one or more of the numerous social units which flourished in Mesopotamia during the second millennium B.C.

Chapter II

THE PATRIARCHAL AGE

THE splendid Third Dynasty of Ur brought great material prosperity to lower Mesopotamia, due to the settled political hegemony which the Sumerians had extended as far as the middle Euphrates. Excavations at Ur have shown the complex nature of contemporary society with its widespread business and commercial dealings, its advanced level of political organisation, and its developed artistic and literary tastes, all of which combined to make life in general very pleasant for the upper and middle classes.[1] One unfortunate result of the vast migratory movements occurring in Mesopotamia about 2000 B.C. was the collapse of the Third Dynasty under the onslaught of the marauding Semitic Martu. Another group, the Amorites, settled in the northern part of the country subsequently known as Assyria. While Babylon and Larsa were struggling for the control of lower Mesopotamia, the Amorites established their capital at Mari (Tell Hariri) and under Shamsi-Adad I (c. 1727-1686 B.C.), a senior contemporary of Hammurabi, they became dominant in the north. The Amorites shared the cultural traditions of Sumer and Akkad, and by the eighteenth century B.C. their influence was so great that they virtually monopolised all the important political positions in Mesopotamia.[2] When Parrot began to excavate at Mari in 1933[3] it became increasingly clear that Amorite culture had kept pace with the military, political and economic developments of the age.

The discovery of an ancient temple dedicated to Ishtar revealed a civilisation which antedated Sargon of Agade (c. twenty-fourth cent. B.C.). A statue which helped to identify the *tell* bore the inscription:

"Lamgi-Mari, king of Mari, high-priest of Enlil, dedicated his statue to Ishtar."[4]

As other shrines were excavated the Sumerian architectural influence became evident, though a departure was noted in the presence of huge guardian animals sometimes fashioned in bronze, and stationed at the doors of the temples. The excavation of the royal palace in 1935 provided fresh evidence of the vitality of Mari culture. Covering a total of one hundred and fifty acres it boasted nearly three hundred rooms, halls and courts,[5] and was in an excellent state of preservation. Some of the original bathrooms contained twin terra-cotta baths, beside which were simple covered toilets.[6] The palace roofs were drained by means of pottery conduits which were found to be in working order some thirty five hundred years after their installation.[7] Tablets recovered from the palace archives included correspondence between Zimri-Lim, the last ruler of Mari, and Hammurabi. The former controlled a vast expanse of territory, and his diplomatic correspondence showed the extent of his contacts with neighbouring monarchs. His military attaches relayed regular intelligence reports from the court of Hammurabi, and one tablet recorded a Mari ambassador as saying:

"Whenever Hammurabi is occupied with any affair, he writes to me, and I go to him wherever he may be. Whatever the affair may be, he tells it to me."[8]

The nomadic Khanu proved to be an unsettling influence in the Mari kingdom, and partly on their account an elaborate system of signalling by fire was developed, enabling news to be flashed to all parts of the state within a very short time.

The place which magic and divination occupied in daily

life was illustrated by the recovery of certain cuneiform texts dealing with hepatoscopy, or liver-examination. Clay models of sacrificial livers had been inscribed with information relating to events consequent upon the sacrifice, and this record served to guide the priest-magicians when confronted with similarly configured livers at future times. Some thirty-two of these models dating to the beginning of the second millennium B.C. were found at Mari.

This phase of Amorite history is of considerable importance for the Patriarchal period. An Elamite-Amorite alliance had brought about the fall of Ur, the original home of Abraham, and it is probable that the Amorites also controlled the region about Haran, to which Abraham and his father migrated. In the Balikh valley south of Haran the names of certain patriarchs were preserved in the designation of sites such as Serug, Peleg and Terah,[9] while Nahor occurred in the Mari tablets as Nakhur, home of some of the Habiru. By the second millennium B.C. the names Abraham, Isaac, Jacob, Laban and Joseph were in common usage. Abraham appeared as *A-ba-ra-ma*, *A-ba-am-ra-ma*, and *A-ba-am-ra-am*, while Jacob (*Ya'qub-el*) was found as a Palestinian place name by 1740 B.C.[10] Used as a personal name Jacob (*Ya-ah-qu-ub-il*) was found on tablets from Tell Chagar Bazar in northern Mesopotamia dated about 1725 B.C.

The cuneiform texts also mentioned an aggressive group of nomads known as the Banu-Yamina or "sons of the right", one of whose chiefs was killed by Zimri-Lim. The description of this marauding band has led some scholars to connect them with the Benjaminites of Genesis[11] on philological and other grounds.[12] It may be noted in passing that the word rendered "chieftain" in the Mari account of the Benjaminites is the term *dawidum*, which is probably the original form of the name David.

Another Mesopotamian cultural centre of great importance for an understanding of the Patriarchal age was the

Horite city of Nuzu (Yorgan Tepe), excavated by Edward
Chiera from 1925. Some twenty thousand clay tablets
written by Hurrian scribes in the native Babylonian
language were unearthed from the family archives of
several villas in the city, and on translation were found
to have preserved a remarkable record of the social and
legal structure of Nuzu culture. While most of the texts
are dated in the fifteenth century B.C., which is somewhat
later than the Biblical patriarchs, they cast a remarkable
light on the life and times of Abraham, Isaac and Jacob,[13]
setting them accurately against the background of second
millennium B.C. Assyrian society.

One of the legal tablets from Nuzu dealt with the activities
of the mayor Kushshiharbe (*c.* 1500 B.C.), who accepted
bribes, indulged in immoral behaviour, used workers on
public projects for his own purposes, and was closely
associated with a group of kidnappers. Ultimately the
outraged citizens preferred charges against him, and he
was brought to trial for his misdeeds.[14] The bulk of the
texts, however, consisted of private or family documents,
some of which mentioned the Habiru contracting on an
individual basis for service as slaves in wealthy households.

Many tablets dealt in some manner with the social
institution of adoption. Because Nuzu law prohibited the
sale of land, real property frequently passed from one
person to another under the guise of adoption proceedings.
An individual could be adopted in this way by numerous
families, to whom he would give a "filial gift" for the privilege of acquiring their estate. Genuine adoptions by childless
couples with a view to perpetuating their family estate
were also common, and even a slave might be adopted for
this purpose. In return the individual thus honoured was
expected to perform normal filial duties and attend to
mourning rites on the death of the parents. Most contracts
of this kind contained a clause to the effect that if a natural
son was subsequently born to the adopting couple, he

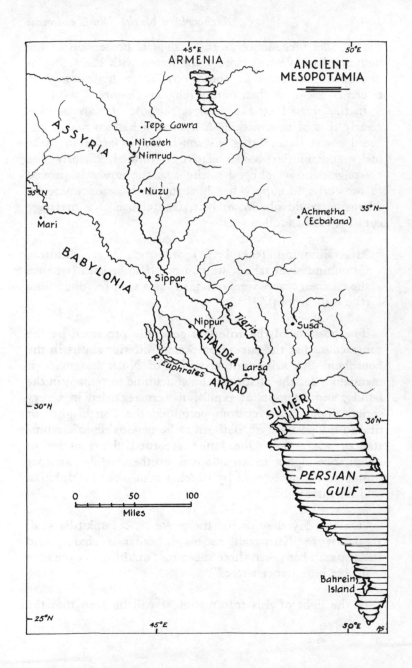

ANCIENT
MESOPOTAMIA

ARMENIA

ASSYRIA

•Tepe Gawra
•Ninaveh
•Nimrud

•Nuzu

35°N

Achmetha
(Ecbatana)

35°N

•Mari

BABYLONIA

•Sippar

Nippur
•
CHALDEA

R. Tigris

•Susa

R. Euphrates
AKKAD

•Larsa

SUMER

30°N

30°N

PERSIAN
GULF

0   50   100
Miles

25°N

Bahrein
Island

45°E

50°E

45

should take precedence as the real heir. Possession of the household gods[15] was closely connected with the rights of primogeniture, so that these terra-cotta figurines were esteemed for more than purely religious reasons.[16]

In the Nuzu texts the primary purpose of marriage was clearly that of procreation. A man who had no male heirs could resort to adopting his son-in-law in order to make his grandchildren blood-relatives. Quite frequently the marriage contract obliged a wife who subsequently proved to be sterile to supply her husband with a concubine by whom he could obtain an heir. One clause of a marriage contract read as follows:

"If Gilimninu (the bride) will not bear children, Gilimninu shall take a woman of N/Lullu-land (whence the choicest slaves were obtained) as a wife for Shennima (the bridegroom)."[17]

The position of the wife was generally protected by the contract so that the concubine was of inferior status in the household. An important provision of Nuzu law made it mandatory for the offspring of a concubine to remain in the family, and attempts at expulsion were regarded in a very serious light. Local custom permitted the "birthright" or title to the position of firstborn to be negotiable as circumstances warranted. One tablet recorded the transfer of inheritance rights to an adopted brother, whilst another contained the agreement by which a man named Tupkitilla sold his birthright:

"On the day they divide the grove . . . Tupkitilla shall give it to Kurpazah as his inheritance share. And Kurpazah has taken three sheep to Tupkitilla in exchange for his inheritance share."[18]

In the light of this information it will be seen that the

Patriarchal narratives of Genesis reflect the social background of Mari and Nuzu with remarkable consistency. Terah migrated with his family from the Persian Gulf to Haran (spelled Harran in the cuneiform texts) about the beginning of the nineteenth century B.C., at a time when northern Mesopotamia was under Amorite control. The adoption practices of Nuzu evidently guided Abraham in his choice of Eliezer as his heir presumptive,[19] clarifying the legal implications of the Divine assurance that Eliezer would not in fact be the true heir. When Sarah continued childless she gave her Egyptian slave Hagar to Abraham as a concubine[20] so as to provide an heir, Ishmael. But when Sarah subsequently bore Isaac the natural son received the rights of inheritance, and the continuing presence of Ishmael in the household was deemed a threat to the position of Isaac. Abraham was most apprehensive[21] when Sarah determined to expel Hagar and Ishmael because such action was in direct contravention of Nuzu law. However, Sarah could have appealed in defence to the ancient Sumerian law-code of Lipit-Ishtar (*c.* 1850 B.C.)[22] which stated that the freedom received by a dispossessed slave was adequate compensation for the act of expulsion.

The transfer of the birthright from Esau to Jacob[23] reflected contemporary Nuzu social customs, which frequently entertained other equally uneven transactions. To the present, however, it is impossible to say whether the traditions of Nuzu permitted the sale of a birthright to a complete stranger, as all recorded transactions are of an inter-familial nature.

A satisfactory explanation of the relations between Jacob and Laban is now forthcoming as a result of the discoveries at Nuzu. Laban apparently had no male heir when he adopted Jacob, and as was usual at the time he gave him his daughters for wives after a designated period of service had been completed satisfactorily. The agreement included a clause that Jacob would forfeit his inheritance rights if he married any other women. A tablet from Nuzu of a similar nature reads as follows:

"The adoption tablet of Nashwi, son of Arshenni. He adopted Wullu, son of Puhishenni . . . When Nashwi dies, Wullu shall be heir. Should Nashwi beget a son (the latter) shall divide equally with Wullu but (only) Nashwi's son shall take Nashwi's gods. But if there be no son of Nashwi's, then Wullu shall take Nashwi's gods. And (Nashwi) has given his daughter Nuhuya as wife to Wullu. And if Wullu takes another wife he forfeits Nashwi's land and buildings . . ."[24]

From the way in which Laban proclaimed his patriarchal rights[25] Jacob was evidently accepted as a legally adopted son, not merely a son-in-law. Under these conditions the wives of Jacob were still the legal property of Laban, and thus were not free to leave the parental household. Within a twenty year period[26] sons were apparently born to Laban, thereby depriving Jacob of the inheritance rights and an accompanying double portion of the estate. When Rachel stole the household gods[27] which were the property of the natural rather than the adopted son, she did so in order to secure the advantages of inheritance for her husband. While the fugitives were legally guilty in leaving the abode of Laban without permission, there was clearly fault on both sides. That Laban had scarcely been an ideal father is seen from the complaint of his daughters,[28] and the entire incident reflects typical oriental intrigue, with each party seeking desperately to extricate himself from a delicate and involved situation.

In Nuzu society imminent death provided the supreme occasion for the bestowal of patriarchal blessings, a practice which is found also in Genesis.[29] These pronouncements constituted the last will and testament of the dying man, and as such were irrevocable[30] and legally binding. Unexpected courses of action frequently resulted, as may be inferred from one legal tablet in which the plaintiff succeeded in maintaining his right to marry a certain woman who had been "willed" to him by his dying father:

"My father, Huya, was sick and lying in bed, and my father seized my hand and spoke thus to me: "My other older sons have taken wives, but thou hast not taken a wife, and I give Zululishtar to thee as wife."[31]

There are still some modern writers who assert that the mention of the camel in the Patriarchal narratives is anachronistic.[32] While it is true that the use of camels as regular beasts of burden was only completely developed by the twelfth century B.C., there can be no doubt that the camel was an important means of transport during the Patriarchal period. Thus an eighteenth century B.C. cuneiform tablet from Alalakh in northern Syria contained a list of fodder for domesticated animals in which the camel (GAM.MAL) was specifically mentioned.[33] When Parrot was excavating Mari he discovered camel-bones in the ruins of a house belonging to the pre-Sargonic era (c. 2400 B.C.),[34] while a relief from Byblos in Phoenicia, dated in the eighteenth century B.C., depicted a camel in a kneeling position.[35] Finally, recently discovered cylinder seals from northern Mesopotamia dating from the Patriarchal era showed riders seated upon camels.[36] In view of the manner in which archaeological excavations in Mesopotamia have demonstrated the existence of a social organisation characteristic of that portrayed in the Patriarchal records[37] there is every ground for belief that the narratives in question have a firm historical basis. As though that were insufficient, the topography of the Patriarchal sagas has been found to be in essential harmony with what is known of the Middle Bronze Age (c. 1900-1600 B.C.) in Canaan.

While the Patriarchs are presented in Genesis as nomadic shepherds or herdsmen[38] they must not on that account be thought to have been uncouth or uncivilised. A contemporary Egyptian relief (*c.* 1900 B.C.) from a tomb at Beni Hasan depicted a group of Semitic semi-nomads visiting Egypt.[39] The men were bearded, while the women held their long hair in place by means of bands. Their clothes were multi-coloured, the men wearing short skirts and sandals, whereas the women had long dresses which they fastened by a clasp at the shoulder[40] and had shoes on their feet. This attire may have appeared a little bizarre to the fastidious Egyptians, but it was by no means primitive, and furnishes an excellent idea of how Abraham and and his contemporaries must have looked.

The Patriarchs were associated with sites in the thickly-wooded hill country of Palestine.[41] Dothan, Gerar, Shechem and Bethel were all inhabited at this time (*c.* 2000-1700 B.C.), as the work of Glueck in the Hashemite kingdom of Jordan has shown.[42] Although the antiquity of Hebron and Beersheba has not been determined as yet, the former was founded "seven years before Zoan in Egypt"[43] while the wells at the latter site are unquestionably of great age.

The political atmosphere of the period is aptly conveyed by the story of Sinuhe, a prominent Egyptian nobleman who lived in the twentieth century B.C. At this time southern Syria and Palestine relinquished tribal organisation in favour of the city-state, while Transjordan became increasingly depopulated and in the end reverted to a tribal system.[44] Political upheaval followed the death of the Egyptian pharaoh Amenemhet I, and Sinuhe fled to Palestine to seek asylum. His "Tale"[45] described the hazardous crossing of the Egyptian border and the hardships experienced en route to Kedem,[46] where he was befriended by an Amorite chieftain of the same kind as Abraham, Laban and Jacob. Ultimately Sinhue became chief of a large Amorite tribe which he commanded in a series of raids and campaigns. His description of Amorite life matches closely that experienced by the Patriarchs, while his estimate of the Palestinian highlands is reminiscent of Deuteronomy:[47]

> "There were figs in it, and vines,
> More plentiful than water was its wine,
> Copious was its honey, plenteous its oil;
> All fruits were upon its trees.
> Barley was there, and spelt,
> Without end all cattle . . ."[48]

In the days of Abraham the five cities of the plain south of the Dead Sea were thriving communities, but their destruction as described in Genesis[49] depopulated the territory. Archaeological investigation has corroborated the general facts of the situation, and Albright has shown that most probably Sodom, Gomorrah and Zoar are beneath the waters at the southern extremity of the Dead Sea, thus precluding excavation by conventional methods.[50]

Gezer, one of the great contemporary Canaanite cities, was excavated by Macalister from 1902.[51] From the strength of the fortifications and the presence of Egyptian statues and other artefacts dated *c.* 1900 B.C. it may be concluded that Gezer was an Egyptian outpost in the Patriarchal period. Megiddo, another site of great strategic importance, was first explored in 1903[52] and subsequently excavated from 1925. The Early Bronze period was represented by a stout defensive wall some thirteen feet thick, later increased in dimensions to almost double the original size. A number of Egyptian objects were recovered from the site,[53] and the excavation of three rectangular temples furnished important evidence of Canaanite religious practices in the days of Abraham. Behind the temples, which were adjacent to one another, was the sacrificial "high place". At the base of the steps on the east side of the pagan altar was a large quantity of animal bones, constituting the residue of the sacrificial offerings made to the Canaanite deities.

The discovery of the Hittite legal code at Boghazköy in Turkey has thrown light on the sale of the Cave of Machpelah.[54] On that occasion Abraham purchased the property from Ephron the Hittite for an apparently exorbitant price. Under ancient Hittite law the one who purchased the entire property of the vendor was under legal obligation to render certain feudal services with the transfer of the land. But if only part of the property was purchased these duties, whose nature is unknown, were not mandatory. Hence Abraham expressed his interest in only a part of the estate so as to avoid any obligation,[55] but Ephron, who obviously found it advantageous to be rid of the property as a whole, would not agree to this arrangement,[56] thus compelling Abraham to become legally feudatory. The sale was conducted in public, and the purchase price was weighed out in silver in accordance with contemporary custom. The mention of trees[57] reflects the Hittite practice of listing the exact number of trees growing on each piece of property sold.[58]

It is sometimes alleged by historians[59] that references to Philistines in the Patriarchal sagas are anachronistic. However, if the term 'Philistines' is extended to include Minoan and other Aegean peoples, they are mentioned in an eighteenth century B.C. Mari tablet, which recorded that a king of Hazor in Palestine sent gifts to Crete (Kaptara).[60] Furthermore, Middle Minoan pottery has been recovered from the seaport of Ugarit (Ras Shamra),[61] from Hazor,[62] and in Egypt from Abydos and Memphis.[63] A long series of migrations which established the inhabitants of Caphtor and others in Palestine had commenced well in advance of 1600 B.C., so that by the Amarna period (fifteenth and fourteenth centuries B.C.) the Philistine settlements in Canaan experienced no linguistic difficulties whatever in dealing with the native inhabitants.[64]

During the Mari age the Amorites frequently ratified treaties by the sacrifice of an ass. This procedure, or *khayaram katalum* as it was phrased in the texts, was an essential feature of agreements between individuals and nations alike. One government official wrote to Zimri-Lim:

> "I sent that message to Bina-Ishtar (and) Bina-Ishtar replied as follows: 'I have killed the ass with Qarni-Lim and thus I spoke to Qarni-Lim under the oath of the gods: "If you despise(?) Zimri-Lim and his armies, I will turn to the side of your adversary".' "[65]

The custom survived in Canaan amongst the semi-nomadic stockbreeders of Patriarchal and later times, and in particular was favoured by the descendants of Shechem, who were known as the "Bene Hamor" or "sons of the ass".[66] They claimed as their deity the Canaanite Baal-Berith or "Lord of the Covenant", and during the conquest of Canaan they were incorporated by means of a treaty into the Israelite peoples.

It will be clear from this general survey of contemporary archaeological material that the Patriarchal sagas are set against a well-authenticated background of non-Biblical sources. As Professor Albright has remarked:

> "Abraham, Isaac and Jacob no longer seem isolated figures, much less reflections of later Israelite history; they now appear as true children of their age, bearing the same names, moving about over the same territory, visiting the same towns (especially Harran and Nahor), practising the same customs as their contemporaries."[67]

Chapter III

ISRAEL IN EGYPT

ABOUT the time that the Neolithic settlers were draining and irrigating the mud flats of Sumeria, the earliest predynastic peoples of Egypt were moving in the direction of community life. The sites of Deir Tasa, Badari and Nagada in Upper Egypt have furnished important information about the beginnings of civilised life and the expansion of agriculture during the fifth millennium B.C. The rough pottery and primitive living conditions of the Tasian period[1] were succeeded by a more sedentary type of culture at Badari about 4000 B.C.,[2] whilst the predynastic period as such (c. 4500-2900 B.C.) was ushered in by the Amrateans, who were probably the first to attempt systematic cultivation of the Nile valley.[3] They were succeeded culturally by the Gerzeans of Lower Egypt who commenced the process by which the land was divided into "nomes" or regions, each of which had a sacred plant or animal as its cult-emblem.

Upper and Lower Egypt were unified by Menes of Thinis,[4] marking the beginning of the Protodynastic period (c. 2900-2700 B.C.). During this time trade was established with the Near East, and Mesopotamian culture began to make an impact upon the Two Lands.[5] The highly developed nature of the Old Kingdom period (c. 2700-2200 B.C.) was typified by the construction of the huge pyramids, which involved prodigious feats of engineering and craftsmanship.[6] With the end of the Sixth Dynasty came a degree of political and social instability which lasted for about two centuries. But the glory of Egypt revived under the leadership of Amenemhet I, founder of the Twelfth Dynasty, who ushered in the Middle Kingdom period (*c.* 2000-1780 B.C.). Upper Egyptian territorial borders were expanded southwards into Nubia, and society in general was organised along feudal lines. The mineral wealth of the Sinai peninsula was developed, and trade relations between Egypt and the Semitic nomads of Canaan and Arabia were expanded.[7]

The political strength of the Middle Kingdom waned in the Thirteenth and Fourteenth Dynasties, paving the way for foreign domination of the Two Lands by the Hyksos, a people of mixed Semitic-Asiatic descent.[8] The subjugation of Egypt about 1700 B.C. by these "Foreign Rulers" was described by Manetho[9] as follows:

"There came unexpectedly men of lowly birth from the eastern regions, who marched in, confident of victory against our land. By sheer weight of numbers they subdued it without striking a blow. Having over-powered our rulers they burned our cities savagely, demolished the temples of the gods, and treated the inhabitants in a hostile manner. They slew some of them, whilst the wives and children of others were made slaves . . ."[10]

The Hyksos were probably of west-Semitic stock in the main, as is indicated by such names as *Ya'qob* and *'Anat-har*, which are Canaanite.[11] An advance group apparently occupied the Delta region about 1715 B.C., followed about 1680 B.C. by the main body who overwhelmed the opposing Egyptians. Their military success was due largely to the introduction of the horse-drawn iron chariot and the strong compound Asiatic bow as weapons of war. When Egypt had been subdued the Hyksos organised feudal city-states in Canaan, and built stone fortifications at Jericho, Shechem, Hazor and elsewhere which frequently housed their chariotry. With the expansion of trade in

Palestine and Syria there arose a patrician class which monopolised wealth and sponsored the development of cultural and artistic movements.[12]

The extent to which Hyksos influence was felt in the Near East is indicated by the presence of relics inscribed to King Khayana in such distant places as Crete and Mesopotamia. For a capital the invaders chose the strategic site of Avaris in the Nile Delta,[13] from which they dominated Egypt for nearly a century and a half. The massive fortifications at Avaris have been excavated and found to conform to the general pattern of Hyksos defence-works. Even more important for this period, however, was the recovery of a *stele* dated about 1320 B.C., and erected by order of Rameses II (*c.* 1290-1224 B.C.) to commemorate the four hundredth anniversary of the founding of Avaris,[14] thus furnishing a date of *c.* 1720 B.C. for the beginning of formal Hyksos rule.

The scribal explanation in Numbers[15] associating Hebron (known to the Patriarchs as Mamre) and Zoan implies that some of the Hebrews were involved in Hyksos enterprises and were in Egypt when Avaris was founded.[16] A further connection between the Hebrews and Egypt may be seen in the prediction of Genesis 15:13, which spoke of a four hundred year affliction for the seed of Abraham.[17] When connected with the reference in Numbers it is a cogent argument for associating the Patriarchal movements with the Avaris era.

Since the Egyptians were normally hostile to the ambitions of enterprising immigrants, the dramatic rise to power of the Semite Joseph can be explained most satisfactorily in terms of a period of Hyksos rule. If elements of the Habiru were involved in some manner with the Hyksos it would have facilitated their entry into Egypt during the Amarna age.[18] The Joseph narratives indicate that the land of Goshen was near the Egyptian capital and that the Hebrews had ready access to the

royal court. Since Thebes in Upper Egypt was the capital
of the Two Lands both before and after the Hyksos
period,[19] the location of Avaris as the seat of government would accord well with the conditions described
in Exodus.

Further evidence of a relationship between the Patriarchal
migration to Egypt and the Avaris era is supplied by the
reference to Joseph buying up the land for pharaoh during
the years of famine.[20] This procedure resulted in the
displacement of the old landed nobility and the creation
of a new class of serfs, reflecting closely the social upheaval
in Palestine under Hyksos rule. In the light of this
and other evidence there seems to be good reason for
assuming that Jacob and his family entered Egypt about
1700 B.C., when the country was under the control of
Semitic foreigners.[21]

Against this background it would not be surprising
to find considerable local colour in the Joseph narratives.
The phrase "overseer over his house"[22] is a direct translation of a title used of officers in Egyptian noble houses,
whilst the designations which indicated that Joseph was
"over my house"[23] and "father to pharaoh . . . lord of
all his house . . . ruler throughout all the land of Egypt"[24]
correspond precisely to the office of Prime Minister or
Vizier of Egypt.[25] The titles "chief of the butlers" and
"chief of the bakers"[26] are familiar from Egyptian inscriptions. The royal birthday procedures including the release
of prisoners,[27] the place accorded to magic in Egyptian
life,[28] the general attitude towards Asiatic semi-nomads,[29]
the one hundred and ten years of Joseph as the Egyptian
ideal of a fruitful and happy life,[30] and the embalming
of Jacob and Joseph[31] were all characteristic features of
contemporary Egypt.

A mural from the reign of Seti I (*c.* 1308-1290 B.C.)
depicted the king investing his vizier with a gold chain.[32]
Riding in chariots, following the Hyksos custom, was

reserved for important state personages, and the ordinary people were required to stand respectfully as the chariot passed.[33] In the tomb of Rekhmire, vizier of Thotmes III, a mural was discovered which depicted slaves making bricks from Nile mud and adding chopped straw and sand. An accompanying inscription read, "The rod is in my hand; be not idle."[34] That periodic famines were not uncommon in Egypt is illustrated by an inscription on the tomb of an official named Ameni (*c.* 1980 B.C.) at Beni Hasan:

"Then came years of famine. Then I ploughed all the acres of the province. I nourished the pharaoh's subjects. I looked after their food, so that there was none hungry among them."[35]

An even more pertinent inscription from the standpoint of the Joseph narratives was found in the tomb of Bebi, a vizier of the Sixteenth Dynasty, at El Kab:

"I collected corn as a friend of the harvest god. I was watchful at the time of sowing. And now, when a famine arose lasting many years, I distributed corn to the city each year of famine."[36]

The narrative of Joseph and the wife of Potiphar[37] was paralleled by a thirteenth century B.C. romance entitled the "Tale of the Two Brothers". It narrated the attempted seduction of a virtuous man named Bata by the wife of his older brother Anubis. After some suggestive remarks the amorous wife

". . . stood up and took hold of him . . . then the lad (became) like a leopard with (great) rage at the wicked suggestion which she had made to him, and she was very, very much frightened. Then he argued with her, saying: "See here—you are like a mother to me, and your husband is like a father to me . . . What is this great crime which you have said to me? Don't say it to me again!' "38

The tenuous nature of Hyksos control over Upper Egypt was made evident shortly after 1600 B.C., when Sekenenre, prince of Thebes, rebelled against Apophis of Avaris. The struggle was continued by Ahmosis, and about 1560 B.C. the Hyksos capital was overthrown. During the next ten years the hated invaders were driven systematically from the Delta region and compelled to withdraw into Canaan. All possible traces of Hyksos rule were eradicated from monuments, public buildings, inscriptions and the like, despite the benefits which the Hyksos had brought to Egypt.39 Under Ahmosis I of Thebes the New Kingdom period (*c.* 1570-1150 B.C.), one of the most brilliant in the whole of Egyptian history, was ushered in. During the Nineteenth Dynasty Rameses II (*c.* 1290-1224 B.C.) moved his capital from Thebes to Avaris, which had been reconstructed by Seti I, and began to enlarge it. Excavations at the site by Montet uncovered statues, *stelae* and other artefacts bearing the name of Rameses and his successors.40 The Exodus narratives appear to indicate this period of reconstruction in the reference to the building of Pithom and Rameses by Hebrew forced labour.41

An ancient site in the Wadi Tumilat, Tell el-Retabeh, has been identified with Pithom, and excavations have uncovered some of the massive brickwork from the time of Rameses II.42 Since no traces of Eighteenth Dynasty construction or expansion were found at the site it must be concluded that the Exodus tradition refers to the *corvée* in the early days of Rameses II. Tanis was known for two centuries (*c.* 1300-1100 B.C.) as *Per-Re'emasese* or "House of Rameses", and in splendour was second only to Thebes.43 This again is important evidence for

the belief that the Israelites worked on royal construction
projects in the time of Rameses II, and would seem to
point to a thirteenth century B.C. date for the Exodus.[44]

In spite of this, certain archaeological findings have
been adduced for a much earlier departure from Egypt,
placed by some scholars in the fifteenth century B.C.
When Garstang excavated Jericho he concluded that
the city had fallen to the invading Israelites about 1400
B.C.,[45] and from the fact that diplomatic contact between
Jericho and Egypt ceased under Amenhotep III (*c.*
1413-1377 B.C.), he formed the view that the Exodus
occurred under Amenhotep II (*c.* 1436-1422 B.C.).

Other scholars have appealed to the Tell el-Amarna
tablets as a means of establishing an early date for the
Exodus. Some three hundred and seventy ostraca were
found by an Egyptian peasant woman in 1887 where
once the city of Akhenaton had stood, and when translated
contained diplomatic communications from Babylonian,
Mitanni and other rulers to Amenhotep III and Akhenaton.
Written in Babylonian cuneiform they dealt with a wide
range of political, social and personal affairs.[46] About one
hundred and fifty originated in Palestine, most of which
complained that the Habiru were overrunning the land,
and requested the immediate aid of pharaoh to maintain
Egyptian control of southern Canaan. One such letter is as
follows:

> "To the king, my lord, say . . . The whole land of the
> king has revolted. There is not one governor that is
> loyal . . . The Habiru are capturing the fortresses of
> the king . . . the Habiru are taking the cities of the
> king . . ."[47]

This material was taken to indicate the conquests of
Joshua as seen from the standpoint of those administrative
officials in southern Palestine who were loyal to the

Egyptian regime,[48] and from this point of view the Habiru were equated with the conquering Hebrews.

A chronological note in Kings[49] stating that Solomon commenced building the Temple four hundred and eighty years after the Exodus furnished a date of about 1441 B.C. for the latter, assuming that Solomon reigned from *c.* 965-925 B.C. Whether this statement is to be taken literally or schematically[50] is not easy to determine, since the reference may involve a double cycle of numerals. If, however, the reference is amenable to a literal interpretation, it argues strongly for a fifteenth century B.C. date for the Exodus.[51]

Whilst neither sequence is wholly free from objections, the archaeological and historical evidence favours a later rather than an earlier Israelite departure from Egypt. Recent work at Jericho has shown the inconclusive nature of the material presented by Garstang, whilst the positive identification of Rameses by Montet[52] has removed all doubt as to whether the "treasure cities" were perhaps built under Thotmes III or Queen Hatshepsut and designated in Exodus by their later rather than their earlier names. Archaeological surveys by Glueck in Transjordan[53] have shown that prior to 1850 B.C. numerous walled cities flourished in the region. But for the next five hundred years an interruption of sedentary occupation resulted in the city-dwellers being replaced by semi-nomadic inhabitants. No subsequent attempt to settle in walled towns was apparent until about 1300 B.C., suggesting that the Israelite conquest of Transjordan did not occur until after that time.

Vincent envisaged a date of about 1250 B.C. for the fall of Jericho, prompted in part by the discovery of some Mycenaean vases at the site. They apparently belonged to the Late Bronze II period (*c.* 1375-1225 B.C.), and had been imported from the Aegean during the Minoan period (*c.* 2000-1000 B.C.). With the bulk of the archaeological evidence weighing heavily in favour of a somewhat earlier date it would appear unwise to rely to any extent upon isolated occurrences of this kind.

One important Egyptian monument precludes a date much beyond 1220 B.C. for the final entry of the Israelites into Canaan. The *stele* of Meneptah (*c.* 1224-1216 B.C.), dating from the fifth year of his reign, narrated his victories over Libya and the eastern Asiatic lands, including Israel:

"Devastated is Tehennu; the Hittite land is pacified;
Plundered is Canaan with every evil;
Carried off is Ascalon; seized upon is Gezer;
Yenoam is made a thing of naught;
Israel is desolated, her seed is not.
Palestine has become a defenceless widow for Egypt;
Everyone that is turbulent is bound by king
Meneptah . . ."[54]

On the *stele* Israel is the only name written with the determinative symbol indicating "people" rather than "land",[55] implying sedentary occupation of western Palestine.

Whilst there are numerous unsolved problems connected with the date of the Exodus and the entrance into Canaan, it would seem most probable that the Israelites left Egypt around 1300 B.C. The route followed can be established with reasonable accuracy now that Rameses has been identified. Considerations of security dictated a journey southeastward to Succoth so as to avoid the frontier fortress of Zilu, which guarded access to the "way of the land of the Philistines".[56] The multitude assembled under Moses between Migdol and the sea, where they were overtaken by the Egyptians. The crossing of the Red Sea has been beset with misunderstanding owing to an incorrect rendering of the Hebrew name *Yam Suph*, which should be translated "Reed Sea" or "Marsh Sea". Thus the names "Red Sea"[57] and "the sea"[58] most probably indicate an ancient lake of reeds situated between the Bitter Lakes and the town of Zilu (Thiel). The oceanic Gulf of Suez can hardly be meant since reeds do not grow there. Thirteenth century B.C. Egyptian sources mentioned a vast papyrus marsh near Tanis,[59] and the actual crossing may have been made somewhat north of the Bitter Lakes, where similar terrain was to be found.

The precise route taken by Moses has been a matter of some debate, since certain sites, including Mount Sinai, are not clearly identified. Other places, however, are fairly assured, such as Elim[60] (Wadi Gharandel), Dophkah[61] (the Egyptian mining centre of Serabit el-Khadem), and Rephidim[62] (Wadi Rephayad). Biblical tradition located the Kenites quite accurately to the south and east of the Gulf of Aqabah. "Kenite" means "belonging to the copper smiths", and the tribe was probably attracted to the Sinai copper mines, worked from the predynastic period,[63] for economic reasons. The Kenites were of Midianite stock, and were amongst the earliest nomadic Bedouin to popularise the use of the camel as a general beast of burden. However the Israelites appear to have been restricted to ass-nomadism, and as such the traditional route of the wilderness wanderings kept them close to the desert oases and the grazing lands south-west of the Dead Sea.[64]

In the Sinai peninsula Moses received a Divine revelation which culminated in the establishing of Israel as the Covenant People. When this agreement was ratified[65] Moses was given directions for the construction of a portable shrine known as the Tabernacle,[66] where the Ark of the Covenant was located and where the congregation of Israel could meet for worship and guidance. The Ark was housed in a part of the shrine to which access was limited, and was made of acacia wood richly ornamented with gold and silver. In it were deposited a number of sacred objects connected with Hebrew worship, including the tablets of the Law. To emphasise the function of the Tabernacle as the focal point of community religion a colourful rectangular enclosure of about twelve hundred square yards surrounded the shrine, and within this area all public services were held.

Such shrines were by no means unknown in antiquity, as indicated in the fragmentary Phoenician histories of Sanchuniathon (*c.* seventh century B.C.), which referred to a portable shrine pulled by oxen. A bas-relief from the time of Rameses II showed the tent of the divine king placed in the centre of the Egyptian military encampment.[67] Other representations of shrines carried by camels occur from Roman and pre-Islamic times.[68] In the light of this evidence it is incorrect to assign structures such as the Tabernacle to a post-Mosaic period, since they were of desert origin and in any event foreign to sedentary Canaanite custom.[69]

Because Israel constituted a special religious community the concepts of Law and Covenant were of particular importance. Due to the discovery of Babylonian, Assyrian and Hittite legal codes, the legislation of Moses appears in much clearer perspective. The Code of Hammurabi is now known to be a comparatively late development in Mesopotamian jurisprudence, being antedated by the codes of Lipit-Ishtar[70] and Eshnunna.[71] The latter, which was drawn up almost two centuries before the time of Hammurabi, contains the first exact parallel to early Biblical law.[72] Hittite legislation followed the pattern adopted by Hammurabi,[73] and may have been codified about 1300 B.C. The enactments reflect the general concepts of justice and order which prevailed throughout the Near East in the second millennium B.C., but gave greater status to womanhood and displayed a more humanitarian spirit than that of the *lex talionis* inherent in the Codes of Moses and Hammurabi.[74]

It is now clear that detailed legal codes such as those found in the Pentateuch are not anachronistic, as was formerly supposed. Nor is it any longer necessary to assign the origin of many Mosaic enactments to the eighth or seventh centuries B.C., for Pentateuchal and other Near Eastern legislation must now be envisaged against a background of a common intellectual and cultural heritage, from which an understandable similarity of antecedents emerges. Despite this, however, striking differences point to an absence of direct borrowing on the part of the Hebrews, as indicated by the Deuteronomic divorce law which permitted a man to put away his wife[75] but did not extend a comparable privilege to a married woman, unlike the Babylonian code.[76]

The covenant relationship between God and Israel has been examined recently in the light of second millennium B.C. international treaties.[77] Such legal undertakings between a great king and a vassal commenced with a preamble which identified the author of the covenant and furnished his credentials.[78] This was followed by an outline of the historical relations between the contracting parties[79] with emphasis upon the integrity of the great king and his graciousness towards his vassal.[80] Then came the obligation to be imposed upon and accepted by the vassal, including a prohibition against the latter engaging in foreign alliances.[81] A further provision stipulated that the document should be in the deposit of the vassal and read publicly at intervals.[82] A concluding portion listed the deities as witnesses[00] and enumerated the blessings or curses which would occur according as the covenant was kept or violated.[84]

Even more important than the provision by the Covenant of a nucleus about which Israelite historical and spiritual tradition could develop is the fact that the Hebrews were unique in antiquity for their attempts to interpret their entire national life in terms of a solemn covenantal relationship with a single Deity. While it reflected many features of contemporary legal agreements, the bond of union between God and Israel which was forged at Sinai was undergirded by concepts of ethical monotheism whose nature was completely foreign to the peoples of the ancient Near East.

Chapter IV

THE SETTLEMENT IN CANAAN

THE organisation of Hebrew life in terms of Law and Covenant was a necessary prerequisite to the occupation of the Promised Land, with all its lurking temptations. Only when the harrassed refugees from Egypt had been welded by the hardships and trials of a generation in the Sinai wilderness into a people of advanced spiritual vision did the work of Moses draw to an end. Shortly before his death the Israelites moved towards southern Canaan, but their entry into Transjordan along the "King's Highway"[1] was halted by opposition from the Edomites.[2] As Glueck has shown, this compact kingdom was defended in the thirteenth century B.C. by strategically-placed fortresses to the west, east and north.[3] To avoid this danger the Israelites apparently skirted the western border of Edom, crossed the river Arnon (Wadi Mojib) and entered the Amorite territory of Gilead. Victories against Sihon and Og gave the Israelites a foothold in Transjordan, and despite the activities of the Babylonian diviner Balaam[4] they encamped in Moab, where Moses died.

At this time Canaan was organised as a series of city-states which were run on feudal lines. The local princes were subject to Egyptian jurisdiction but had their own chariotry and infantry[5] for use in times of danger. The corruption of Egyptian bureaucracy resulted in an administrative and social decline in Canaan, which may have contributed somewhat to the rapidity with which the Israelites occupied the territory. The unsettled nature of the times can be appreciated from a perusal of the Amarna tablets originating in Canaan, a number of which complained about the marauding Apiru. Because of the close relationship between this name and the designation "Hebrew", some scholars have associated the activities of the Apiru with the Israelite invasion of Palestine.[6] However, the Amarna ostraca refer to the Apiru as lawless bands of discontented mercenaries, and in another connection to kings who were engaged in raiding and seizing neighbouring cities. There is no mention of an invasion of Palestine as such, and the tablets merely seem to speak of local unrest in Canaan.[7]

Whatever inkling Joshua may have had of these conditions, his first consideration was to gain access to the land by overthrowing the Hyksos fortification of Jericho, which dominated the entrance to the Jerusalem plateau. This ancient site has been extensively excavated since 1907, when Sellin and Watzinger explored it,[8] followed in 1929 by Professor Garstang.[9] Work was resumed at Jericho in 1952 under Kathleen Kenyon,[10] whose findings indicated that Jericho was one of the oldest inhabited sites in the Near East, with an occupational history going back to the fifth millennium B.C. The pre-pottery Neolithic inhabitants had constructed a huge defensive ditch about thirty feet wide, which had been cut laboriously some eight feet down into bed rock. Surrounding the ditch was an eighteen foot wall surmounted by a circular stone bastion, a structure which constitutes the earliest-known city fortification.

Unfortunately the most recent work throws very little light on the period of Joshua, and contrasts strongly with the findings of Garstang, who believed that he had found ample evidence of destruction under Joshua about 1400 B.C. His excavations uncovered a fifteenth century occupational level (City D) which he described as fortified with a massive double wall of brick, the outer structure being about thirty feet high and six feet thick, whilst the inner one was much the same height but over twice the thickness. This fortification had replaced the formidable stone bastion and brick rampart of a previous Middle Bronze Age II city (*c.* 1700 B.C.). The debris resulting from the destruction of the site suggested a great conflagration, probably resulting from seismic disturbance.[11]

The work of Miss Kenyon has shown that the walls which Garstang ascribed to "City D" dated from the third millennium B.C., and were part of a complex defensive system erected during that general period. As a result virtually nothing can be said about the nature and extent of Jericho in the time of Joshua, and it may be that the once-powerful Hyksos fortress had become little more than an outpost by about 1300 B.C.,[12] though still imposing in appearance.

Excavations at the sites of Ai, Bethel, Lachish and Debir have furnished positive evidence for their destruction in the thirteenth century B.C. Ai (et-Tell), some thirteen miles north-west of Jericho, was excavated by Madame Marquet-Krause in 1933 and found to have been one of the major fortresses in Canaan between 3200 and 2400 B.C. The site was completely destroyed about 2300 B.C., and remained unoccupied except for a modest village settlement about 1100 B.C.[13] It was thus in ruins at the time of the Hebrew conquest, and the name Ai or "ruin"[14] may have been given to it at that period.[15] This can hardly be the city which was reduced to a *tell* during the second phase of the conquest,[16] and it has been suggested that the misunderstanding arose because the inhabitants of Bethel, a mile and a half distant, occupied Ai as an advanced base to halt the attack of the Israelite invaders.

Bethel was excavated in 1934 under Professor W. F. Albright, and shown to have been a prosperous city in the Middle and Late Bronze Ages. During the thirteenth century B.C. it was destroyed by a tremendous conflagration which deposited a solid mass of ashes and debris on the site.[17] Albright concluded that the sack of Bethel was associated with the ruins of Ai by a subsequent generation.[18] If the suggestion made by Vincent[19] is correct that Ai was a military outpost on the edge of Bethel, and if its destruction was connected with the simultaneous overthrow of a nearby site, there may be sufficient reason for the account being subsumed under the narrative of the victory at Ai.[20]

Archaeological activity at Lachish (Tell ed-Duweir)[21] began in 1933 under J. L. Starkey, who demonstrated the Early Bronze Age origins of the site. Under the Hyksos it became an important fortified post, and in the time of Joshua it was controlled by an Amorite governor. Three Canaanite shrines were built in the Hyksos chariotry enclosure between the fifteenth and thirteenth centuries B.C., and when excavated revealed a number of cult-objects, storerooms and places for sacrificial worship.[22] Large quantities of animal bones were unearthed in a pile of debris, and on examination most of them were found to have come from the right foreleg of the animal.[23]

A fragmentary bowl from Lachish proved when reconstructed to date from the thirteenth century B.C. It was inscribed with a notation, perhaps made by an Egyptian tax-collector, dealing with wheat deliveries from local harvests. An accompanying date mentioned the fourth year of a pharaoh whose name was not given. The Egyptian script was contemporary with Merneptah, *c.* 1224 B.C. Since the bowl was broken when the city was destroyed it would appear that Lachish fell between 1220 and 1200 B.C.[24]

In Late Bronze Age levels at Lachish a bowl and a jar were found, on which were inscriptions in an early Canaanite script identical with the proto-Sinaitic characters of Serabit el-Khadem first discovered by Petrie,[25] and

PLATE 4. The Taylor Prism of Sennacherib.
A cuneiform chronicle of events in the reign of the Assyrian
monarch Sennacherib (*c.*705-681 B.C.)

PLATE 6. Babylonian Chronicle Tablet.
This fragment contains the account of the capture of Jerusalem by Nebuchadnezzar's forces on March 16th., 597 B.C.

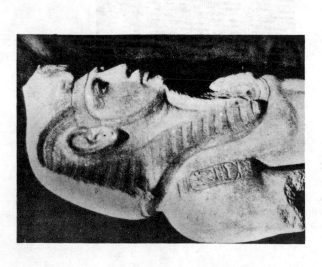

PLATE 5. Meneptah of Egypt (*c.* 1230 B.C.)
A celebrated pharaoh whose exploits in Canaan and the East were recorded on the Meneptah *stele.*

similar to Late Bronze Age specimens from Shechem, Gezer and Beth-shemesh. These ancient Hebrew writings constitute an important link with the earliest known Phoenician forms upon which the later Greek and Roman alphabets were based.[26]

Once Lachish and Eglon (Tell el-Hesi) were in Israelite hands, the main attack from the lowlands was pressed against Hebron and Debir. The latter site (Tell Beit Mirsim), thirteen miles south-west of Hebron, was excavated by Kyle and Albright from 1926.[27] A charred layer of debris some three feet thick in places separated subsequent Hebrew occupational levels from the Late Bronze Age remains underneath. A royal scarab of Amenhotep III which was unearthed helped to date the destruction of the city at about 1200 B.C.[28] Excavations at Beth-zur[29] showed that the site had been abandoned at the time of the Hyksos expulsion from Egypt, and was reoccupied only about 1200 B.C. It is of some significance that the houses and fortifications of Palestine which date from this period (Early Iron Age) show a marked cultural deterioration, which would accord with the general outlook of the Israelites on their entry into Canaan.

The third stage in the occupation of the land was accomplished with the destruction of Hazor, the principal city of the Galilee region.[30] Apart from a few soundings made at the site (Tell el-Qedah) by Garstang in 1926, nothing was known archaeologically about the Galilee campaign of Joshua. The *tell* covered about twenty-five acres, and stood on the highway leading from Egypt to Syria, Anatolia and Mesopotamia. Just north of it was a huge rectangular plateau about one hundred and seventy-five acres in area and protected by an earthen defensive wall some fifty feet high, which Garstang had identified as an enclosure for Hyksos chariotry. An expedition from the Hebrew University of Jerusalem under Dr. Y. Yadin began to excavate the mound and the plateau from 1954,[31] and discovered that the last city had covered both the mound and the enclosure. An estimate of the population showed that about forty thousand people were living in Hazor at the time of the Israelite conquest.

The antiquity of the location was indicated by the earliest of the seventeen occupational levels excavated, which was dated about 4000 B.C. The rampart surrounding the enclosure was found to be contemporary with Hyksos deposits. In the middle of the camp enclosure a cemetery dating from the Middle and Late Bronze Ages was uncovered, and this indicated that the last occupation of the site terminated during the thirteenth century B.C., not about 1400 B.C., as Garstang had suggested.[32] If the evidence of destruction at the Late Bronze Age levels of various Palestinian sites is to be correlated with the campaigns of Joshua, therefore, it would appear that the land was occupied comparatively quickly. This would substantiate the Biblical assertion that while the territory as a whole had fallen to the invaders,[33] certain sites such as Bethshan,[34] Taanach, Megiddo and the Jebusite stronghold of Jerusalem still remained to be possessed.[35]

Two second millennium B.C. cultures must now be considered in the light of the influence which they exerted over Canaan prior to the Israelite conquest. The Middle Bronze Age (*c.* 1900-1600 B.C.) witnessed the first Indo-European migration from the Caucasus to penetrate the uplands of Cappadocia.[36] These peoples were known as the Hittites, and may have included Hurrians and some Hivites. They intermingled with the ancient Khatti of Anatolia, whose territory they conquered, and set up a number of city-states. Whilst it is not always clear whether the early Biblical references[37] are to the early Khatti or the later Hittites, there can be no doubt as to the antiquity of the culture which was first unearthed by Winckler at Boghazköy (Khattusas) in east-central Asia Minor.[38] Large numbers of clay tablets were found, and when the various languages were deciphered the grandeur of Hittite history began to be revealed.

The earliest period of Hittite power commenced about 1850 B.C., at a time when the ancient Assyrians exercised military control in upper Mesopotamia. Fifty years later the Old Empire was established by Pitkhanas, king of Kussar, and after two centuries the Hittite kingdom extended from Syria to the Black Sea. Internal strife under Mursilis I (*c.* 1600 B.C.) weakened Hittite influence and led to an expansion of the old Mitanni kingdom of northern Mesopotamia under the Hurrians. But with the accession of Suppiluliuma (*c.* 1395-1350 B.C.) the New Empire period of Hittite history began, and the Mitanni kingdom was reduced to the position of a buffer state between Asia Minor and Assyria. Suppiluliuma extended his military interests to the Lebanon range, and established friendly relations with Egypt. One of his letters to Amenhotep III (Huria) read in part:

"Thus hath Suppiluliuma the great king, king of Hatti-land, to Huria, king of Egypt, my brother, spoken: 'I am well. With thee may it be well . . . just as thy father and I mutually requested presents, so wilt also thou and I now be mutually good friends'."[39]

The New Empire period began to wane under Hattusilis III (*c.* 1275-1250 B.C.), and the decline of Hittite power was hastened by intrigue in the confederate states. By the time the invasion of the Aegean "Sea Peoples" had left the Philistines in firm control of the Palestinian coast somewhat after 1200 B.C., the once-powerful Hittite empire had passed from the historical scene.

Tablets recovered from Boghazköy have furnished dramatic evidence concerning the virility of Hittite civilisa-

tion and its influence upon the general development
of ancient Near Eastern culture. Cuneiform texts have
demonstrated that the Hittites controlled the smelting
of iron ore and the manufacture of iron for all trading
purposes up to the end of the New Empire period.
They were renowned horsemen, and were the first to
manufacture the iron chariot and introduce it as a weapon
of war.[40] Hittite society was based on an agricultural
economy, and the legal codes have preserved complicated
title-deeds containing inventories of estates.[41] From two
Royal Addresses it appears that the relatives of the
king monopolised the highest offices of state, and that
the Hittites enjoyed a prolonged tradition of settled court
life.[42] From an examination of cuneiform sources Gurney
has concluded that the Empire constituted an exclusive
caste superimposed on the indigenous population, which
in earlier days had consisted of a number of separate
townships ruled by a body of elders.[43]

Fragmentary legal tablets unearthed at Khattusas were
found to contain several closely related collections of
laws. These may indicate the various stages in the
development of a legal corpus, since the main series
speaks of a "former" penalty whereas other tablets state
that the king has "now" prescribed a different, usually
less severe, punishment.[44] The legislation envisaged the
same general concepts of justice as those enshrined in
the Code of Hammurabi and other Near Eastern legal
systems. The inviolable nature of oaths, covenants and
treaties was emphasised, and in contrast with the Mosaic
and Hammurabi codes the principle of retaliation was
subordinated to that of restitution. As mentioned previously, the advanced nature of Hittite legislation appears
in the marked respect shown for the status of womanhood.[45]

Hittite religion was of a highly syncretistic nature,
and its pantheon included Sumerian, Akkadian and

Egyptian deities as well as the nature-gods of the Hatti. Religious shrines varied from comparatively simple open-air sanctuaries to the elaborate Cyclopean structures at Boghazköy. The latter followed the Babylonian custom of grouping a number of small rooms around a central paved court, but whereas the Babylonian inner shrine was linked directly with the courtyard, thus affording the worshippers a clear view of the proceedings, the Hittite holy place (*cella*) was approached by an indirect route, suggesting that comparatively few worshippers were present in the inner shrine.[46] Civil and administrative functions appear to have been connected with the Hittite temples as with their Babylonian counterparts. In the official pantheon the sun goddess was known as "Queen of the Land of Hatti, Queen of Heaven and Earth, mistress of the kings and queens of the Land of Hatti, directing the government of the King and Queen of Hatti". Her husband was the Weather deity of Hatti whose cult was widespread throughout Anatolia.

This "King of Heaven, Lord of the Land of Hatti" claimed the daily ministrations of the temple priests, who attended to his "physical needs" in the matter of food, clothing, entertainment and the like. Propitiatory offerings were brought to him and animals were sacrificed to secure his blessing. Occasional instances of human sacrifice have been reported from the cuneiform texts,[47] and on all occasions they appear to have been offered under special circumstances. Religious festivals included a spring rite for re-invigorating the earth and a ceremony held at the vernal equinox in which the king frequently participated.[48] As in Mesopotamia magic and divination occupied a large place in human affairs.[49]

The other important culture of the second millennium B.C. was that of Canaan, which was far in advance of its counterpart in Israel during the period of the

Judges. The Canaanites had taken advantage of the technological changes ushered in at the end of the Bronze
Age, and whilst still employing copper and bronze for
many common purposes they turned increasingly to
iron for weapons of war, agricultural implements and
a wide variety of architectural needs. The Canaanites
were a trading nation, and shared with the Philistines
the Egyptian import and export trade. In the Judges
period the Philistines became the dominant political and
social influence, having asserted their strength by destroying Tyre, Sidon, Ugarit and other coastal cities
after being repulsed in a naval battle off the Egyptian
coast by Rameses III (*c.* 1180-1149 B.C.).

Much information about the Canaanites has been
forthcoming from discoveries at Ras Shamra (Ugarit),
where a rich tomb was accidentally discovered in 1928.
The site was excavated by Schaeffer from 1929[50] and
found to date from the Neolithic period. It was known
as Ugarit in the second millennium B.C., and as such
was mentioned in Egyptian and Hittite texts. During
the fourteenth century B.C. Ugaritic culture reached
its height, after which time it fell successively under
Hittite and Egyptian influence.

In the ruins of a building located between two temples
at Ugarit were found thousands of clay tablets written
in an unfamiliar cuneiform language. When deciphered
the script was found to be alphabetic rather than syllabic,[51]
whilst the language itself claimed a close affinity to Phoenician
and Biblical Hebrew. Ugaritic texts included poetry
and prose,[52] the former consisting of mythological cycles
and legends whilst the latter reflected the highly developed
nature of Ugaritic society in describing land-ownership,
diplomatic affairs, taxation, civic administration, veterinary
practice and many other topics.

The king was the divinely appointed leader of society,
whose task was to ensure justice and equity. Following

Hittite traditions the army was composed of infantry, archers and charioteers, with the addition of several priests as staff astrologers.[53] Whilst the tribe was still basic to social organisation, the town was becoming increasingly important for administrative purposes. Social customs concerning land tenure and adoption were similar to those obtaining in Mesopotamia, and the educational system also followed the same general pattern.

Whilst the menace which the Canaanites constituted in the area of religion is familiar from the Old Testament, the true nature of Canaanite cult-worship has become much clearer within recent years. Most of the poetic texts from Ugarit deal with Canaanite deities and heroes, the former presenting such fluidity of function and personality that their exact relationships are very difficult to determine on occasions. The cult was essentially a debased form of ritual polytheism which was associated with particularly lewd and depraved orgiastic procedures. The supreme Canaanite deity was El,[54] the "father of man" (*abu adami*) and the "father of years" (*abu shanima*), who was depicted on a *stele* with hands outstretched in blessing over the ruler of Ugarit.[55]

The consort of the god El was Asherat, known to Israelite tradition as Asherah, and their offspring was the fertility-deity Baal (Haddu), the overlord of rain and storm.[56] His titles included the names Aliyn (*The Prevailer*) and Zabul (*Earthly Lord*), the former being prominent in Ugaritic poetry. It is now clear from a perusal of the texts that Baal is neither a generic name for a number of local deities, as was formerly supposed, nor yet a spirit which, in association with a particular territory, developed the functions of a vegetation-god. Instead Baal must be accorded the status of a true "high god", a cosmic deity who was the acknowledged head of the Ugaritic pantheon. Such texts as the Baal and Anat cycles[57] have preserved religious rituals which are strongly reminiscent of the Egyptian ceremonies associated with the cult-worship of Isis and Osiris. Quite incidentally, the account of Phoenician mythology as preserved by Eusebius from Philonic sources has been shown to be correct in large areas of detail.[58]

The prose and poetic compositions from Ugarit exhibit grammatical and literary forms which are also found in parts of the Hebrew Bible, notably the Psalter, and their discovery has done much to clear up alleged textual anomalies.[59] Many passages formerly regarded as corrupt are now seen to exhibit peculiarities of Canaanite grammar and linguistic expression whose significance had lapsed with the passing of the centuries. As with the Hebrew Psalms literary parallelism was conspicuous in Ugaritic poetry, as for example,

> "Lo, thine enemies, O Baal,
> Lo thine enemies wilt thou smite.
> Lo thou wilt vanquish thy foes."[60]

which is similar to the thought of Psalm 92:9,

> "For behold thine enemies, O Lord,
> For behold thine enemies shall perish.
> All the workers of iniquity shall be scattered."

Further consonance in the matter of linguistic and idiomatic expressions appears in the description of Baal as the "Rider of the Clouds"[61] who is enthroned in the heavens[62] and hurls down lightning and thunderbolts.[63]

Certain Hebrew social institutions have also been paralleled from Ugaritic writings, as in the case of the blindness which Nahash the Ammonite desired to inflict upon the inhabitants of Jabesh-gilead.[64] An equivalent passage in the legend of Aqht described king Daniel invoking blindness upon the town in which his son had been murdered:

> "Woe unto thee, City of Mourners
> Near which Aqht the Hero was smitten!
> May Baal make thee one-eyed
> From now and unto eternity . . ."[65]

The reference in Psalm 74:13f. to "dragons" and "leviathan" recalls the Ugaritic legend of Baal and Anat, where the sea-monster Tannin was invoked for magical purposes.[66] Such Hebrew allusions to Canaanite mythology are few, however, and in general it would appear that Biblical poetry is less stylised and more spontaneous than its Ugaritic counterpart, whilst from a theological standpoint there is a complete divergence in thought. The morality of God as expressed in early Hebrew legislation was completely lacking in Canaanite thought, which frequently portrayed the lowest depths of moral depravity. Ritual prostitution was a popular feature of Canaanite religion, and representations of Anat depicted her as a divine courtesan. The lily and the serpent, commonly found in association with the fertility-goddess, were symbols of fecundity.[67] In another text Anat was represented as a butcher, slaying young and old alike in a fiendish orgy,[68] reminiscent of Egyptian sources which characterised Anat and Astarte as deities of violence and war and showed them naked astride galloping horses, waving battle weapons.[69]

For the most part Canaanite worship was carried out at the "high places", which seem to have been outdoor altars located on or near the tops of hills.[70] To these shrines the worshippers brought the produce of their fields or sacrificial offerings from their flocks. The ritual which was normally followed included prayer and the presentation of votive offerings, and was concluded by a sacrificial feast at which the deity was entertained as host or guest. Certain parts of sacrificial animals were considered the perquisite of the deity and were burned upon the altar.[71] Ugaritic religious texts indicate that Canaanite sacrificial ritual was considerably more diversified than its Israelite counterpart,[72] and according to the Old Testament records there were specific cult-objects associated with sanctuary worship. One of these was the *asherah*, a sacred grove, tree or wooden emblem connected closely with the mother-deity Asherah.[73] Another was the sacred pillar, which may have been a representation of a male deity.[74]

Small altars of incense were commonly found at Canaanite sanctuaries after 1100 B.C., as for example at Megiddo, where the best current example of an altar of burnt offering was also uncovered.[75] The incense altars were made of limestone and had projections or "horns" on each corner. One such altar found at Palmyra in north Syria had the word *hammanim* or "altar of incense" inscribed on it.[76] Excavations at Lachish revealed the ruins of a Canaanite temple at thirteenth century B.C. levels, which appeared to have been destroyed whilst still in use as a shrine. Although the walls had sustained heavy damage by fire, they showed clear indications of having been plastered and lined with benches for storing sacrificial offerings. A raised platform at the front of the structure had probably accommodated an idol and perhaps a small altar. To the rear of the building were clearly-defined storage areas and small rooms for the priests. Debris from the sacrifices indicated that four types of animals had been offered, and the almost complete absence of burned bones showed that the sacrificial meat had been boiled.[77]

Whilst in the light of these discoveries there can be little doubt that Canaanite culture had a profound effect upon many aspects of Hebrew life, it is equally clear that in the area of religion there could be little compromise between the ideology of Israel and the paganism of Canaan if both were to retain their true characteristics. The nature of Canaanite cult-worship as indicated in the Ugaritic texts is patently one of the utmost moral depravity. Its barbarity and licence had a peculiar appeal to contemporary peoples, and its demoralising influence even penetrated the highly conservative religions of Babylonia and Egypt. Its sordid nature was the very antithesis of the ethical monotheism for which the Sinai covenant stood, and the expression of its religious fervour in terms of ritual prostitution, snake worship, child sacrifice and licentious behaviour could never be espoused by the truly moral Israelite, as the spiritual leaders of the pre-exilic period emphasised continually.

The destruction of Megiddo in the third quarter of the twelfth century B.C. has thrown some light on the dating of the Song of Deborah.[78] This ancient poem celebrated with great vigour the Israelite defeat of the Canaanite oppressors. References to the "waters of Megiddo" and the "river Kishon"[79] denoted the stream which arose in neighbouring springs and flowed round the site of Megiddo. Yet the battlefield was located at Taanach, some four miles to the south-east and not at Megiddo, the most powerful fortress in the plain of Esdraelon. The explanation for this is that the Canaanites were conquered at a time when Megiddo lay in ruins and Taanach was the nearest inhabited site with which the victory could be associated. This would indicate that the Song of Deborah is to be dated about 1100 B.C., before Megiddo was rebuilt.[80]

The general picture of the history, culture, geography and religion of Israel as presented in the Book of Judges seems amply borne out by recent archaeological discoveries, and is consistent with the Palestine of between 1200 and 1000 B.C. One significant difference between

Israel and her pagan neighbours should be noted, however, and this lay in the realm of political organisation.[81] Whereas Israel was at best merely a loose confederation of tribes united by a common loyalty to the Sinai covenant, the neighbouring peoples were constituted as monarchies or city-states governed by local kings. As a result of the almost complete lack of a central authority the Israelites were virtually defenceless before the marauding Ammonites, Moabites, Midianites and Philistines. This situation was partially remedied by the charismatic leadership of the "Judges",[82] but the rise of inter-tribal misunderstandings[83] and the seductive attractions of Canaanite religion furnished powerful forces for disunity and disintegration, prompting the demand for a regularised monarchy.[84]

Chapter V

FROM MONARCHY TO EXILE

A GOOD deal of information relating to political, social and religious conditions in the early days of the monarchy has emerged as the result of archaeological activity at Gezer, Beth-shemesh and elsewhere. Gezer was excavated by Macalister from 1902[1] and shown to have had an occupational history going back to about 3000 B.C.[2] The natural rock caverns nearby had been used for burials in the Early Bronze Age[3] and at a later period were dignified by the erection of several rough stone pillars from five to ten feet in height. This suggested to Macalister that the locality had once been a Canaanite "high place", but it is now thought probable that the stones constituted memorials to deceased kings of the city.[4] From tenth century B.C. levels at Gezer came the celebrated "calendar", a small limestone tablet describing the various months of the year and the corresponding agricultural work undertaken:

"His two months are (olive) harvest; his two months are grain-planting; his two months are late planting; his month is hoeing up of flax; his month is barley-harvest; his month is harvest and festivity; his two months are vine-tending; his month is summer fruit."[5]

Beth-shemesh (Ain Shems) to the south east was first excavated in 1911 and revealed an occupational activity extending from 2000 B.C. to 600 B.C.[6] The late Canaanite stage was represented by fine pottery artefacts, weapons and scarabs. Here was found one of the many plaques in honour of Canaanite goddesses, depicting a female figure surrounded by serpents. Though Beth-shemesh was apparently in Israelite hands when the Philistines captured the Ark of the Covenant[7] about 1050 B.C., the culture of the city was predominantly Philistine.

When Gibeah (Tell el-Ful) was excavated by Albright[8] there came to light a fortress which represented the second occupation of the site, the first town having been destroyed in the Judges period.[9] This fortress probably served as the headquarters of Saul during the Philistine campaign, and was located on the summit of the *tell*. A casemate defensive wall of a type introduced into Syria by the Hittites surrounded the citadel, which in appearance must have resembled Shechem, Beth-shemesh and Tell Beit Mirsim (eleventh to tenth centuries B.C.),[10] whose walls are comparable in structure and design. The two-storey building at Gibeah was serviceable rather than luxurious,[11] and the remains of pottery vessels and a plough suggested continuous agricultural activity in the general area. This would imply that Saul was more of a rustic chieftain than a king in the Solomonic sense.

An iron ploughpoint unearthed from the *tell* and assigned to *c.* 1010 B.C. is the earliest dateable iron implement so far recovered from the Palestinian uplands, and is important in the light of the monopoly which the Philistines exercised over the manufacture and distribution of iron.[12] At the close of the Hittite New Empire period (*c.* 1200 B.C.) iron was esteemed almost as highly as gold and silver. When the Philistines inherited the Hittite smelting techniques about 1100 B.C. they controlled the distribution of iron implements in Palestine, thus thwarting the economic growth of Israel. This barrier to material prosperity was only removed when David broke Philistine power.

The tradition which associated King David with music

and psalmody has been verified by archaeological discoveries, which indicate clearly that for centuries previously Palestine had been noted for its musical interests.
The Beni Hasan tableau depicted visiting Palestinian
nomads walking behind their animals in Egypt to the
accompaniment of a lyre,[13] while Egyptian monuments
from 1550 B.C. referred to examples of Canaanite music.[14]
Ugaritic texts were replete with religious poetry, some
of which parallels the phraseology of the Hebrew Psalter.
These cuneiform sources also furnish references to a
class of temple personnel known as "Sarim",[15] similar
to the Hebrew singers of the monarchy and later times.
Some of the servants of David who were engaged
in this activity possessed Canaanite names such as Heman,
Chalcol and Darda,[16] designated "sons of Mahol", *i.e.*
members of the orchestral guild,[17] and regarded as native
Canaanites.[18] At Megiddo the treasure room of the royal
palace contained large numbers of gold, ivory and alabaster
objects typical of twelfth century B.C. Canaanite culture.
The excavators uncovered one plaque inlaid with ivory
showing a royal personage seated upon a throne and
drinking from a small bowl. Before him stood a musician
plucking the strings of a lyre.[19]

The rise to power of King David[20] necessitated the
selection of a capital in neutral territory so as to unite
the northern and southern tribes. The ultimate choice
was the Jebusite stronghold of Jerusalem, which was
considered impregnable by the native defenders. The
site had been occupied from 3000 B.C., and as early
as 2000 B.C. was mentioned by name in Egyptian texts.
The city was built on a limestone promontory known
as Ophel, where excavators have uncovered very old
fortifications[21] consisting of massive walls, bastions and
gates which were apparently Jebusite in origin.

Being deficient in water supplies the site depended
upon underground cisterns and reservoirs. The nearest

source was the spring of Gihon in the Kedron valley
south-east of Ophel, and in order to gain ready access
to this supply the Jebusites had tunnelled through the
rock to bring the water under Ophel into a deep cistern
some forty feet below ground level.[22] Another structure
designed to channel water from Gihon consisted of a
long aqueduct which emptied into the "old pool"[23]
just outside the city walls. This conduit was only partly
tunnelled, and was stopped up by King Hezekiah prior
to 701 B.C.

Whilst it would have been possible for the followers
of David to have entered Jerusalem by means of this
or another tunnel, it would have been a formidable
undertaking. An alternative possibility has been furnished
by Albright[24] who showed that the word *cinnōr*, translated "water-shaft" or "gutter" is a Canaanite word
meaning "hook", implying that access to Jerusalem was
gained by means of grappling hooks. Under David the
capital city was populated by royal retainers, and being
outside tribal jurisdiction it owed allegiance to the king
alone. An analysis of Assyrian provincial records shows
that the Davidic empire extended from the Gulf of Aqabah
to the Pass of Hamath,[25] whilst other sources indicate
that his bureaucracy was organised along Egyptian lines.[26]

Biblical tradition regarding the age of Solomon has
received similar confirmation in recent years as the
result of archaeological activity.[27] During the reign of
this notable monarch Phoenicia was one of the major
powers in the Near East, and Solomon was quick to
avail himself of Phoenician skills and experience in
his constructional and commercial enterprises. As an
administrative procedure he divided the country into
twelve regions,[28] and imposed direct taxation in the
form of weighed silver, goods, or unpaid labour. The
widespread use of the camel as a beast of burden had
led to an established caravan trade between southern

Arabia and the Fertile Crescent,[29] and by obtaining control of the frontier districts of Damascus, Hawran, Ammon, Moab and Edom it became possible for Solomon to monopolise the entire caravan trade within a very short time.[30] His commercial dealings with Egypt and Cilicia in horses and chariots[31] also attained a high level of prosperity.

With Phoenician aid Solomon built a large fleet of merchant ships based at Ezion-geber on the Red Sea, just south of Edom. These vessels journeyed to Ethiopia and south-west Arabia once in three years,[32] bringing back a cargo of gold, silver, ivory, apes and baboons.[33] The "fleet of Tarshish" also carried smelted metal from colonial mines in the western Mediterranean, which accords with contemporary Phoenician practices as illustrated by inscriptions from Nora and Bosa in Sardinia. These sources indicate that in the ninth century B.C. the Phoenicians had well-established colonies in that area, and were busily engaged in developing the natural resources for commercial purposes.[34]

The explorations of Glueck in the Wadi Arabah have disclosed other aspects of business life in the Solomonic era. The first copper refinery ever found was built for Solomon in the tenth century B.C. by Phoenician workmen, who drew upon a long tradition of skill in the construction of copper furnaces and the refining of ore.[35] Ezion-geber (Tell el-Kheleifeh), situated between the hill-country of Sinai and Edom, was ideal for the purpose since it received the full force of the fierce windstorms blowing down the Arabah from the north. Excavations revealed the presence of an unusual building situated at the north-west corner of the *tell*, and when properly uncovered the walls of this structure were found to contain two horizontal rows of holes in an otherwise blank surface. A series of air ducts ran through the middle of the main walls and were connected to the upper row of holes to form flues. The ore was placed in crucibles inside the smelter and a brush or wood fire, made intensely hot by the draught from the flues, reduced the ore to ingots for shipment elsewhere. While copper ore may have been imported from Sardinia or Spain, there were sufficient deposits of copper and iron[36] in the soft sandstone to permit mining at the site during the days of Solomon. Adjacent to the mines were several small furnaces where the ore underwent preliminary processing, as is indicated by the presence of numerous slag-heaps. Beside them were the ruins of foundry rooms and the living-quarters of the miners themselves, many of whom were probably slaves.[37]

As a result of this technological development the mining industry of the Arabah[38] furnished Solomon with the principal export of his day, thereby adding to his immense wealth. He entered into commercial dealings with the Arabian monarchs, including the celebrated Queen of Sheba (Saba). Whilst the oldest Sabaean inscriptions only go back to about the eighth century B.C., it is known from cuneiform sources that queens ruled over large tribal confederacies in northern Arabia from the ninth to the seventh centuries B.C.[39]

The nature of the ambitious building projects instigated by Solomon is evident from the excavations conducted at Gezer[40] and Megiddo. The latter site was apparently an administrative centre, and in the tenth century B.C. was occupied by a fortified palace. At this time an earlier wall, constructed of finely cut stone piers with a filling of coarse masonry, was replaced by a massive fortification complete with defensive towers. A double outer gateway to the north led to the main inner gate with its huge wooden double doors, behind which were three additional entries protected by guardrooms.[41]

To the south-east was a stable-compound marked by a double row of hitching posts which also served as supports for the roof. Stone mangers stood beside the posts on the cobblestone floors.[42] The district officer of Megiddo had a residence in one of the adjacent towers, while at the opposite end of the city stood another large group of stables fronted by a paved courtyard complete with a drinking trough. The masonry elements of the walls, though typical of the Solomonic era, reflected earlier Phoenician constructional techniques, and appeared in a similar form at Gezer, Lachish and Ezion-geber.[43]

By far the most spectacular public works of the Solomonic era were to be found in Jerusalem. Solomon rebuilt the Millo or defensive station erected by David at the northern end of the old city,[44] and extended the mound of Ophel, at which time he engaged Phoenician craftsmen to design and construct a series of buildings including the royal palace and the Temple. Whilst it is as yet impossible to attribute constructional remains in Jerusalem to the immediate reign of Solomon, contemporary buildings indicate that the Temple was a characteristically Phoenician edifice.[45] The ground plan as described in Kings[46] is very similar to that of the eighth century B.C. chapel excavated at Tell Tainat in Syria.[47] The latter was a rectangular structure with three rooms leading from a portico fronted by two columns. The shrine (*cella*) had a raised platform, and the entire structure was probably lined with cedar.

Examples of the proto-Aeolic pilaster capital used in the Temple have been recovered from eleventh century B.C. levels at Megiddo, Samaria and Shechem, as well as from the eighth century B.C. strata of Megiddo. The lilies and palmettes of the Solomonic temple were typically Syro-Phoenician, while cherubim were commonly encountered in the iconography of western Asia between 1800 and 600 B.C.[48]

Whereas the royal palace took thirteen years to build, the Temple was completed in a matter of seven years. It was a narrow rectangular limestone structure about thirty-five yards long and ten yards wide, and was erected on a larger platform.[49] A flight of ten steps led to the entrance, on either side of which were two free-standing bronze pillars of elaborate design,[50] about thirty-eight feet in height. They may have served as cressets or fire-altars,[51] particularly since they were crowned with a *gullah* or oil-basin for a lampstand.[52] Across the vestibule (*ulam*) was a double door decorated with carving and inlaid with gold leaf which led to the main sanctuary or "holy place". This room, about forty-five feet high, thirty feet wide and sixty feet in length, was floored with cypress and lined with cedar. The flat roof was supported by cedar beams and the walls were decorated with carvings and gold inlay. Beyond this area lay the "most holy place", a cedar-lined thirty-foot cube which housed the Ark of the Covenant, and which was dominated by two olive-wood cherubim covered with gold leaf.

In the courtyard stood a huge bronze altar composed of three stages,[53] with projections issuing from the upper corners. Adjacent to it was a cast bronze laver known as the "molten sea", which was set in position on the backs of twelve bulls oriented towards the quarters of the compass. This enormous object probably weighed about thirty tons, and is eloquent testimony to the metallurgical and engineering skills of the Phoenician craftsmen who designed and executed it. Whilst the structure was used as a laver,[54] the designation "sea" appears to have had mythological associations.[55]

That the Solomonic temple was characteristically Phoenician is also apparent from such features as the shape of the vestibule with its columns, the cedar lining of the interior, the carved and inlaid decorative work, and the insertion of windows immediately below the ceiling.[56] Quite aside from its official significance, it was a monument to the advanced religious syncretism of the age which later fell under the stern condemnation of the prophets of Israel.

With the death of Solomon about 931 B.C. the kingdom separated into two parts, the northern area, Israel, coming under the leadership of Jeroboam, an officer in charge of the Solomonic *corvée* in the north. He fortified Shechem as his capital, and established bull-worship in Dan and Bethel in order to offset the religious influence of Jerusalem. The Canaanites, Arameans and Hittites invariably depicted their deities either standing upright on the backs of beasts or seated on a throne borne by animals,[57] and it may well be that Jeroboam was following the religious traditions of these peoples to some extent in his own cult-worship. Thus he probably intended the golden bulls to serve as a pedestal for the invisible deity, and not to be venerated as objects of devotion in themselves.[58] In the end, however, they were merely one part of the spiritual declension in Israel which was marked by the introduction of fertility-cult groves,[59] high places for Canaanite deities,[60] and other forms of gross idolatry.

Taking advantage of the unsettled conditions in Palestine following the death of Solomon, Shishak I of Egypt invaded Judah in 925 B.C.[61] and removed much of the Temple and palace treasure accumulated by Solomon. That the attack on Judah was part of a larger attempt to reassert Egyptian authority in Asia is clear from the inscription of Shishak on the temple walls at Karnak,[62] which depicted him conquering the Asiatics and leading them captive. His savage Libyan and Nubian troops ranged through the Negev and Transjordan, destroying Debir and Beth-shemesh as they penetrated to the Gilead region. A fragment of a *stele* of Shishak was unearthed at Megiddo, showing the extent of his conquests.[63] When the marauding Egyptians finally withdrew, Rehoboam set about fortifying his frontiers to guard against further invasions from the south, as excavations at such sites as Lachish, Tell en-Nasbeh[64] and Azekah have demonstrated.

Whilst Shishak was campaigning in Palestine, the Aramean dynasty of Damascus was increasing in influence after a rather obscure beginning. The discovery in 1940 of the inscribed *stele* of Benhadad I at a north Syrian site[65] furnished general confirmation of the Syrian list in Kings,[66] but failed to identify Rezon who seized Damascus during the Solomonic period and founded the dynasty. If Rezon is a corruption of Hezion, the name must be excluded from the list in Kings.[67] Since, however, he apparently established the hostile character of the Damascene regime towards Israel, such a procedure seems undesirable.

Before the Benhadad *stele* was discovered it was usual to distinguish at least three Damascus rulers of that name. The first was an ally of Asa; the second, his son,[68] was identical with Adadidri (Hadadezer) who opposed Shalmaneser III from 853 to 845 B.C., whilst the third was a son of the Hazael who murdered Benhadad II[69] and fought against Shalmaneser III in 841 B.C. The Melqart *stele* was left by one of these,[70] and is usually attributed to Benhadad I.[71] Since, however, the *stele* is mutilated in part and the patronymic is lost, it is difficult to be certain about this identification. Bright[72] followed Albright in subsuming the three individuals under the name of Benhadad I, and assigned a forty year period[73] to his reign (*c.* 880-842 B.C.). This must be regarded at the best as tentative, since the *stele* is dated by epigraphy to around 870 B.C., and if Benhadad I died about 860 B.C., his successor, Benhadad II (Adadidri) would then be the contemporary of Ahab. At present, therefore, the evidence of the *stele* must be regarded as less than decisive in this matter.

The notorious dynasty of Omri (*c.* 880-873 B.C.)[74] saw a resurgence of Israelite power and renewed trade

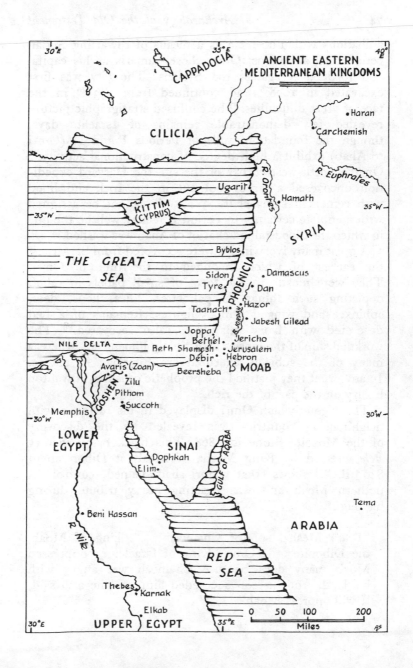

ANCIENT EASTERN
MEDITERRANEAN KINGDOMS

CAPPADOCIA

CILICIA

Haran
Carchemish

R. Euphrates

Ugarit

R. Orontes

Hamath

35°W

KITTIM
(CYPRUS)

SYRIA

THE GREAT
SEA

Byblos

Sidon
Tyre

PHOENICIA

Damascus

Dan

Hazor

Jabesh Gilead

Taanach

JORDAN

Joppa

Bethel

Jericho

NILE DELTA

Beth Shemesh
Debir

Jerusalem
Hebron

Avaris (Zoan)

Beersheba

MOAB

Zilu
Pithom

GOSHEN

Memphis

Succoth

30°W

LOWER
EGYPT

SINAI

GULF OF AQABA

Dophkah

Elim

Tema

Beni Hassan

ARABIA

R. Nile

RED
SEA

Thebes
Karnak

Elkab

0   50   100   200

UPPER   EGYPT

Miles

30°E

35°E

affiliations with Phoenicia as a means of thwarting Syrian commercial ambitions. Omri chose Samaria as his capital and fortified it against the Syrians. The city was first excavated in 1908[75] and continued from 1931[76] in the face of great difficulties. The confused stratigraphic picture revealed few demonstrable remains of Israelite days, though the foundation walls of Periods I and II (Omri to Ahab) exhibit a high degree of constructional activity.[77] On the north-west corner of the site the Harvard expedition uncovered a large pool cut in the rock and lined with cemented stone slabs. Whilst it cannot be assigned with complete certainty to Period I, it may well be the one in which the bloodstained chariot of Ahab was washed.[78]

A great many ivory inlays were recovered from Samaria,[79] the earliest of which belonged to the time of Omri. They were mostly in the form of small panels in relief, depicting such things as palmettes, lilies, lions, deer, sphinxes and winged human figures. Remains of a bed decorated with ivory inlay were also recovered.[80] The workmanship of the ivories is distinctly Phoenician, whereas many of the subjects executed are Egyptian in nature. In any event they justified the prophetic censures of wanton luxury on the part of the rich.[81]

The vigour which Omri displayed in his relations with neighbouring countries was revealed by the discovery of the Moabite Stone in 1868. This black basalt victory *stele*, erected by King Mesha of Moab at Dibon about 840 B.C., shows that Omri had gained control of nothern Moab and was exacting heavy tribute during his reign:

"I am Mesha, son of Chemosh . . . king of Moab, the Dibonite . . . Omri, King of Israel . . . oppressed Moab many days because Chemosh was angry with his land. And his son succeeded him, and he also said, 'I will oppress Moab' . . ."[82]

At this time some contact was established with the Assyrians, for Israel was subsequently referred to in cuneiform records as *Bit-Humri,* a designation which was also applied technically to Samaria the capital city. The royal successors were known as *mar-Humri* or "offspring of Omri".[83]

Under Ashurnasirpal II (*c.* 883-859 B.C.) the Assyrian military power became the terror of neighbouring countries, and the Assyrian texts boasted of the brutalities and atrocities which their armed forces committed:

"I flayed all the chief men who had revolted, and I covered the pillar with their skins; some I walled up within the pillar, some I impaled upon the pillar on stakes, and others I bound to stakes round about the pillar; many within the border of my own land I flayed, and I spread their skins upon the walls; and I cut off the limbs of the officers, of the royal officers who had rebelled . . ."[84]

Shalmaneser III (*c.* 858-824 B.C.) continued the policy of expansion and aggression begun by his father Ashurnasirpal II, and in 853 B.C. he engaged in battle at Kharkar on the Orontes with a coalition of twelve Syrian kings. The Monolith Inscription of Shalmaneser gave an account of the battle, which is not mentioned in the Old Testament, and named "Hadad-ezer of Aram" as one of the opposing leaders who commanded a large number of chariots and soldiers. "Ahab the Israelite" was credited with the most powerful military group of the entire coalition,[85] and his inclusion in the list furnishes independent confirmation of his ninth century B.C. rule.

In the eighteenth year of his reign Shalmaneser again attacked a Syrian coalition, but Jehu of Israel chose to pay tribute rather than fight. The famous Black

Obelisk of Shalmaneser, found by Layard in the royal palace at Nimrud in 1846,[86] depicted Jehu kneeling in submission before the Assyrian king and offering gifts:

> "Tribute of Jehu, son of Omri. Silver, gold, a golden bowl, a golden beaker, golden goblets, pitchers of gold, lead, staves for the hand of the king, javelins, I received from him . . ."[87]

Hazael, who had usurped the Syrian throne[88] resisted the Assyrians, and when they withdrew he subjugated most of Israel and established himself firmly in the Philistine plain. Probably the Solomonic Megiddo was destroyed at this time, since Stratum III represents a complete divergence from its predecessors. Whereas Crowfoot dated the casemate[89] walls of Samaria in Period I (Omri to Ahab) because of the careful constructional patterns followed,[90] Albright dated it in Period III (Jehu) and envisaged the destruction of the fortifications as the work of Hazael. The ceramic evidence suggests that Periods I, II and III at Samaria followed at close intervals, making the remains more difficult to date. At all events the stout walls and large cisterns discovered by the excavators furnished clear evidence of the ability of Samaria to withstand a siege, whether by the Syrians[91] or the Assyrians.[92]

The northern kingdom reached the height of its material prosperity under Joash (*c.* 798-781 B.C.) and Jeroboam II (*c.* 781-743 B.C.), as indicated by the rebuilding of the royal palace at Samaria (Period III). This structure was dominated by a strong rectangular tower, and was built from limestone blocks. The jasper seal of "Shema, servant of Jeroboam", discovered by Schumacher at Megiddo in 1904[93] is probably to be assigned on epigraphic grounds to this period,[94] and the magnificently executed lion which it depicts is a fitting testimony to the artistic standards of the eighth century B.C.[95] Whereas stamp and cylinder seals were used for marking personal property in Mesopotamia as early as the Ubaid and Uruk phases[96] and similarly employed from the Old Kingdom period in Egypt, the earliest inscribed Israelite seals of certain date are found in the days of Jehu.[97]

To the reign of Jeroboam II must be assigned the famous Samaritan ostraca.[98] Some sixty-three potsherds inscribed in ink were recovered in 1910 by the Harvard expedition in some ruins just west of the royal palace.[99] When deciphered they proved to consist of administrative documents recording shipments of wine and oil to Samaria. One potsherd contained the name of the treasury official in receipt of the wine, the district from which it had been dispatched, and the names of the peasants who had paid their taxes in this manner. Of the twenty or more place-names mentioned, six[100] appear as clan designations in the Old Testament.[101] One such tablet reads:

"In the tenth year. To Shamariah from Beeryam, a jar of old wine.

Raga, son of Elisha	2
Uzzah . . .	1
Eliba	1
Baala, son of Elisha	1
Jedayah	1"[102]

The "pure clarified wine" and the refined oil typified the exaggerated demands of the luxury-loving Samaritan elite, and provoked the stern rebukes of the prophet Amos.[103]

After usurping the Assyrian throne about 745 B.C., Tiglathpileser III began to subjugate Syria and Palestine. Menahem of Israel paid tribute to him,[104] and the Assyrian annals recorded that:

"As for Menahem, terror overwhelmed him . . .
he fled and submitted to me . . . silver, coloured
woollen garments, linen garments . . . I received as
his tribute . . ."[105]

The powerful Assyrian ruler appeared once again
on the Israelite scene in response to an appeal by
Ahaz of Judah (c. 731-715 B.C.) for help against a
threatened attack by a Syrian-Israelite coalition.[106] After
receiving a present of Temple and palace treasures from
Ahaz, Tiglathpileser III marched against the alliance,
captured Galilee, besieged Damascus, occupied the Philistine plain and took considerable numbers of prisoners
into captivity.[107]

Tiglathpileser III was succeeded by Shalmaneser V
about 727 B.C., who besieged Samaria when Hoshea
of Israel (c. 731-722 B.C.) refused to pay the Assyrian
tribute and instead sought to ally with Egypt.[108] Before
Samaria fell in 722 B.C. Shalmaneser was succeeded
by Sargon II (c. 722-705 B.C.), who overthrew the
Israelite monarchy and carried the tribes into captivity.[109]
In the Khorsabad annals he boasted of his achievements:

"I besieged and captured Samaria, carrying off 27,290
of the people who dwelt therein. 50 chariots I gathered
from among them . . ."[110]

Some twenty years later Sennacherib, the successor
of Sargon, invaded Palestine, isolated Tyre and reduced
Joppa, Ashkelon, Timnath and Ekron. An Egyptian
force sent to the relief of the latter city about 701
B.C. was defeated, and the frontier fortress of Lachish
fell under heavy attack. In order to gain a brief respite

Hezekiah offered tribute to Sennacherib,[111] which the Annals described as follows:

> "As for Hezekiah the Jew, who did not submit to my yoke, 46 of his strong walled cities, as well as the smaller cities in their neighbourhood . . . I besieged and took . . . Himself, like a caged bird, I shut up in Jerusalem, his royal city . . . As for Hezekiah, the terrifying splendour of my majesty overcame him . . . and his mercenary troops . . . deserted him.[112]

In order to strengthen the city against a seige, Hezekiah ordered his engineers to construct a tunnel which would convey water from the spring of Gihon into the old city. The conduit[113] was duly excavated through solid rock for nearly six hundred yards, terminating just inside the south-eastern corner of the city, where the pool known in later times as Siloam was situated. This hurried attempt to supplement previous tunnels and reservoirs was all the more memorable because the excavators worked with hand tools from opposite ends, meeting with amazing accuracy in the centre.

The presence of this tunnel was discovered in 1880, and an inscription was found on the right hand wall some twenty feet from the Siloam entrance. Written in eighth century B.C. script (*c.* 701 B.C.) it described the engineering achievement as follows:

> "Now this is the story of the boring through; while the excavators were still lifting up their picks, each towards his fellow, and while there were yet three cubits to excavate, there was heard the voice of one calling to another, for there was a crevice in the rock on the right hand. And on the day they completed the boring through, the stone-cutters struck

pick against pick, one against the other; and the
waters flowed from the spring to the pool, a distance
of 100 cubits. And a hundred cubits was the height
of the rock above the heads of the stone-cutters."[114]

Unusual palaeographic value attaches to the Canaanite
characters of the inscription because of the scarcity of
contemporary material written in Hebrew. Along with
the notations on potsherds, seals,[115] and graffiti, the
Siloam inscription constitutes an important item in the
rather sparse collection of material available for the Hebrew
palaeographer.[116]

Whilst Sennacherib was at Lachish his military offensive
was under the control of several officials whose titles
alone have survived.[117] The Assyrian monarch was suffi-
ciently gratified by his conquest of Lachish to have a
carved stone panel installed in his palace at Nineveh,
depicting him seated upon a throne receiving the spoils
of victory.[118]

To the present there is no archaeological evidence
for the captivity of Manasseh in Babylon,[119] though
there is a reference to a visit made by him to Nineveh
about 678 B.C. at the command of Esarhaddon:

"I summoned the kings of Syria and those across
the sea—Baalu, king of Tyre, Manasseh, king of Judah . . .
Musurri, king of Moab . . . twenty kings in all. I gave
them their orders . . ."[120]

The discovery of the ancient legal code during renovations
to the Temple fabric in the days of Josiah (*c*. 639-608 B.C.)
suggests that a foundation-deposit had been made when
the Temple was built. This practice was common in
ancient Mesopotamia,[121] and was originated by the
Sumerians. The precise nature of the code is uncertain,
and it may have constituted only a small portion of the

Mosaic law. However, there can be no doubt as to its genuine nature, since it was adopted as the permanent religious legislation for Judah, a step which was unique in the ancient Near East.[122]

Assyrian power reached its height under Ashurbanipal (*c.* 669-630 B.C.), a man of wide cultural pursuits whose library housed as much of the historical, scientific, legal and religious literature of ancient Mesopotamia as his emissaries could accumulate. This valuable store was discovered in 1853, and included tablets of the Baylonian Creation and Flood narratives which were deciphered by George Smith in 1872. When Ashurbanipal died Assyrian power crumbled, and in 612 B.C. Nineveh fell to Babylonian and Medan forces. The Egyptian pharaoh Necho went to Haran to the assistance of the beleaguered Assyrians[123] but was defeated at Carchemish by Nebuchadnezzar in 605 B.C. The Babylonians advanced towards the Egyptian border and made Jehoiakim of Judah tributary.[124] After three years Jehoiakim rebelled, despite the warnings of Jeremiah,[125] and the Babylonian forces swept down on Jerusalem in 597 B.C. The Temple was looted and Jehoiachin, who had succeeded his father a few months earlier, was carried captive to Babylon by Nebuchadnezzar.

The discovery in 1956 by D. J. Wiseman of four additional tablets of the Babylonian Chronicle in the archives of the British Museum furnished the first extra-Biblical account of the capture of Jerusalem, and in addition gave details of the events which took place between 626 and 594 B.C. It is now possible to assign the fall of Jerusalem to the second of Adar (March 15-16) in 597 B.C. with complete accuracy.[126] The Chronicles also recorded the shattering defeat of the Egyptian forces at Carchemish in 605 B.C., and the Babylonian occupation of "the whole area of Hatti".[127] A previously unrecorded battle between the Babylonians and Egyptians took place

in 601 B.C., in which both sides suffered heavy losses
and Nebuchadnezzar was compelled to withdraw to
Babylon for a year in order to obtain new equipment.[128]
The following twelve months were spent in exploratory
attacks in Syria prior to reducing Jerusalem in 597 B.C.
The evidence furnished by the Chronicles thus confirms
the Biblical tradition that Jerusalem fell to the Babylonians
in 597 B.C. and in 587 B.C.[129]

Vivid light has been shed upon the last days of the
kingdom of Judah through the discovery in 1935 of
eighteen ostraca inscribed in the ancient Canaanite script.[130]
These potsherds were uncovered by J. L. Starkey at
Lachish (Tell ed-Duweir) in the ruins of a small guard-
room located just outside the city gate. In 1938 another
three inscribed potsherds were found at the site,[131]
and like their predecessors they consisted of letters and
name-lists from the period immediately preceding the
destruction of Jerusalem in 587 B.C. The bulk of the
ostraca can be dated from the autumn of 589 B.C., since
they belong to the layer of ash representing the final
overthrow of Lachish by Nebuchadnezzar.[132] Although the
sherds are in a bad state of preservation, with only about
one third of the text fairly intelligible, they are of great
importance philologically, quite aside from their significance
for the age of Jeremiah.[133]

Most of the documents consisted of dispatches written
from a military outpost north of Lachish by one Hoshaiah
to a man named Joash, probably a staff officer at Lachish.
Hoshaiah was apparently responsible for interpreting
the smoke or fire signals from Azekah and Lachish
(Ostracon IV)[134] at a time when the

". . . army of the king of Babylon was fighting against
Jerusalem and against all the cities of Judah that
were left, Lachish and Azekah, for these were the
only fortified cities of Judah that remained."[135]

PLATE 8. An Aramaic Papyrus from Elephantine.
This document from an Egyptian garrison town of
the fifth century B.C., lay undiscovered in the
archives of the Brooklyn Museum for a number of
years before being published in 1953.

PLATE 7. The Ishtar Gate of Babylon. A painting by
Maurice Bardin of the reconstruction according
to Unger of the city of Babylon. The Ishtar Gate
is in the foreground, with the "Hanging Gardens"
and the Great Ziggurat in the upper right.

PLATE 9. The First Qumran Cave. Some idea of the difficult terrain can be gathered from this picture of the entrance to the cave in which the Dead Sea Scrolls were first discovered.

PLATE 10. The Thanksgiving Hymns. The scroll is partially unrolled, and in an obviously poor state of preservation.

Ostracon III made mention of a certain "prophet" as follows:

". . . And it hath been reported to thy servant, saying, 'The commander of the host, Coniah, son of Elnathan, hath come down in order to go into Egypt; and unto Hodaviah, son of Ahijah and his men hath he sent to obtain . . . from him.' And as for the letter of Tobiah, servant of the king, which came to Shallum, son of Jaddua through the prophet, saying, 'Beware!' thy servant hath sent it to my lord."[136]

The identity of the "prophet" has been a matter for considerable speculation, with some scholars assuming that Jeremiah himself was being referred to,[137] and others claiming that an unknown contemporary prophet was being quoted.[138] Torczyner identified him with Uriah (Urijah) of Kiriath-jearim, whose rash utterances had precipitated his flight into Egypt, whence he was extradited and executed in Jerusalem.[139]

Ostracon VI contained the complaint of a patriotic official about certain communications sent out by the *sarim* (royal officials and notables) which were having a demoralising effect upon the people:

"And behold the words of the [princes] are not good, (but) to weaken our hands . . . my lord, wilt thou not write to them saying, 'Why do ye this [even] in Jerusalem?' . . . as the Lord thy God liveth, truly since thy servant read the letters there hath been no [peace] for [thy ser]vant . . ."[140]

The charge of "weakening the hands" of the people was, ironically enough, the identical one which was laid against Jeremiah by the *sarim* in the days of Zedekiah.[141]

Few Biblical prophecies have been more vividly illustrated by archaeological discoveries than the Book of
Jeremiah, and it is not too much to say that the Lachish
ostraca represent a highly important "supplement" to
that book.[142]

Chapter VI

EXILE AND RESTORATION

ALTHOUGH the Babylonians had taken Jehoiakin into captivity and had established his uncle Zedekiah as regent, they still regarded the exiled monarch as the rightful king of Judah. Excavations near the Ishtar Gate in Babylon[1] uncovered several tablets which listed the rations of oil and grain allotted to captives living in Babylon between 595 and 570 B.C.[2] In the list of the royal princes was included "Yaukin, king of the land of Yahud",[3] who was mentioned in Kings as a recipient of Babylonian royal bounty.[4] Further evidence of the status of Jehoiakin in Babylon was discovered in the Palestinian Shephelah when three stamped jar-handles were found at Debir and Beth-shemesh.[5] They bore the words, "Belonging to Eliakim, steward of Yaukin",[6] and each impression had been made from the same seal. This would imply that the property of Jehoiakin was kept intact, and that a crown steward named Eliakim supervised it between 598 and 587 B.C.[7]

Another seal, recovered from Tell en-Nasbeh[8] eight miles north of Jerusalem, has furnished the earliest known representation of a fighting cock[9] It belonged to "Jaazaniah, servant of the king", who was a Judaean royal official.[10] A seal impression was also recovered from the ruins of Lachish in 1935[11] and bore the inscription, "To Gedaliah who is over the household". On the reverse side the impression showed traces of the papyrus document to which it had been attached, and which had long since perished. The owner of the seal was undoubtedly the Gedaliah appointed by Nebuchadnezzar as governor of

Judah.[12] The title "who is over the house" was invariably borne by the chief administrative official next in rank to the king. Both the father[13] and grandfather[14] of Gedaliah had been important state personages.

The general area which the exiles occupied in Babylonia can be identified with reasonable certainty as a result of excavations at Nippur. Two cuneiform tablets dating from about 443 B.C. and 424 B.C. referred to an irrigation canal named *naru kabari* or *nehar kebar*, which joined the Euphrates just north of Babylon, flowed through Nippur and was linked with the river once more just south of Ur.[15] The name Tel Abib[16] or "mound of ears of corn" is the Hebrew form of the Babylonian *Til Abubi* or "mound of the flood", apparently a common name in all periods of Babylonian history and found in this form in numerous inscriptions.[17] The actual site of the exilic occupation, however, has not been identified with complete certainty to date.

While the exiles were in Babylonia the regime of the Chaldeans attained the height of its development. Nebuchadnezzar was as interested in the arts of peace as in military conquests, and he set about making his empire the most splendid of all time. Using captives from several countries as forced labour for building and irrigation projects Nebuchadnezzar began to expand and beautify the capital city of Babylon. This ancient "gate of God", probably first built by the Sumerians, had experienced a long and troubled occupational history,[18] but in the New Empire period of Babylonia (*c.* 612-539 B.C.) it became the most magnificent city of the Near East. Excavations at the site under Koldewey from 1899 onwards[19] have revealed something of the splendour boasted of in the Book of Daniel.[20]

The city was enlarged on both sides of the Euphrates, and was surrounded by a heavily fortified double wall reinforced by an additional brickwork barrier.[21] Nine tenths of the total area consisted of parks and gardens, while the remainder was occupied by temples, public buildings and private dwellings. The defensive walls were surmounted by two hundred and fifty towers stationed at regular intervals, and access to the city was gained by means of eight gates. The most celebrated of these was the Ishtar Gate opening on to the wide processional street which was decorated with rows of bulls and dragons executed on the coloured bricks in enamel and gold leaf.[22] Perhaps the most spectacular structure was the huge *ziggurat* which Nebuchadnezzar rebuilt in the temple area, and which, according to Herodotus, consisted of eight stages.[23]

To the east of the processional street lay the royal palace, while on the north-east corner was the probable site of the celebrated "hanging gardens" of Babylon,[24] built by Nebuchadnezzar to remind his Median queen Amyitis of her mountain homeland. The gardens were actually laid out on elevated terraces supported by huge arches, and were irrigated by means of a mechanical hoist which raised the water to the level of the city roofs. Other magnificent public buildings and temples testified to the industry of the period, as recorded in contemporary inscriptions:

"The produce of the lands, the products of the mountains, the bountiful wealth of the sea, within her I gathered . . . great quantities of grain beyond measure I stored up in her. At that time the palace, my royal abode . . . I rebuilt in Babylon . . . great cedars I brought from Labanon, the beautiful forest to roof it . . ."[25]

In this unfamiliar situation the exiles were bidden by a letter from Jeremiah to settle down[26] and endure the penalty of apostasy. Little is known about their living conditions, but from the Book of Ezekiel it is apparent that they exercised a considerable degree of self-government. Worship assumed a new, non-sacrificial character, and house-gatherings for instruction in the Law became prominent.[27] Prayer, confession, and study of the Torah took place on the sabbath,[28] forming the basis of subsequent synagogue worship. Circumcision was stressed as a means of distinguishing the exiled Jews from their pagan neighbours who did not indulge in the rite, and an emphasis upon the native genius of the Hebrew spiritual tradition served to counter the influence of the Marduk cult-worship. While the exiles recognised Jehoiakin as their lawful king, they were compelled by the circumstances to date events not so much by his regnal years as by those of his captivity, a system adopted in the prophecies of Ezekiel.[29]

When Nebuchadnezzar died about 562 B.C. he was succeeded by several weak rulers until Nabonidus (*c.* 556-539 B.C.), the last king of Babylon, came to the throne. He was a cultured individual who restored the temple of the Moon goddess at Ur[30] and maintained a small museum in the precincts, part of which was unearthed by Woolley.[31] He also collected ancient inscriptions and other artefacts from widely separated places in Mesopotamia, and ordered a chronology of monarchs to be compiled.

Before setting out about 553 B.C. for a series of campaigns in Arabia he made his son Belshazzar regent, while he himself, according to cuneiform sources, took up residence at Teima in Arabia and erected lavish buildings there after the Babylonian manner.[32] The reference in Daniel[33] to Belshazzar as the last king of Babylon can now be understood in the light of this evidence. The statement that Nebuchadnezzar was "father" of Belshazzar[34] reflects the common Semitic custom of employing the terms "son" and "grandson" interchangeably in family relationships. In this same connection it should be noted that Nitocris, mother of Belshazzar, was actually the daughter of Nebuchadnezzar.[35]

To date archaeological findings have failed to establish any identification which would resolve conclusively the "elusive problem of Darius the Mede".[36] However the discovery of one of the Nabonidus texts at Haran referring to the "king of the Medes" in 546 B.C. raises the question as to whether this may perhaps have been an alternative name for Cyrus. Thus D. J. Wiseman would translate the Daniel reference[37] as "in the reign of Darius, even in the reign of Cyrus the Persian".[38] An alternative solution based upon cuneiform sources has been proposed by Whitcomb,[39] who noted that most translations of the Nabonidus Chronicle failed to distinguish between two separate individuals, Ugbaru and Gubaru, and instead identified them with the Gobryas of Xenophon[40] who died after the fall of Babylon. Whitcomb suggested that Ugbaru was the governor of Gutium who conquered Babylon in 539 B.C. and died shortly afterwards. Gubaru was then appointed governor of Babylon by Cyrus and ruled the city for about fourteen years, appearing in the Book of Daniel as Darius the Mede. This theory is based on new facts, and makes it clear that Darius the Mede can be regarded as an historical personage, whatever his true identity.

The last days of Babylon were heralded by the dramatic rise to power of Cyrus, king of Anshan, a vassal of Astyages, king of Media. Cyrus revolted against his suzerain in 549 B.C., and three years later defeated Croesus of Lydia, thereby gaining control of Asia Minor. In 539 B.C. he attacked Babylon, and the Cyrus cylinder narrated the way in which Marduk, the patron deity, assisted his attempts to overthrow the proud city:

"Marduk . . . to his city Babylon he caused him

to go, he made him take the road to Babylon, going as a friend and companion at his side . . . without battle and conflict he permitted him to enter Babylon. He spared his city Babylon a calamity . . ."[41]

To the exiled Jews Cyrus was the one whom God had raised up to restore their fortunes,[42] an expectation which was realised in the proclamation of an act of clemency liberating all captives in Babylonia.[43] The Cyrus cylinder recorded the edict which permitted all exiles to return to their homeland:

"From . . . to Ashur and Susa, Agade, Ashnunnak, Zamban, Meturnu, Deri, with the territory of the land of Gutium, the cities on the other side of the Tigris . . . the gods, who dwelt in them, I brought back to their places . . . all their inhabitants I collected and restored them to their dwelling places . . ."[44]

The book of Ezra commenced with an account of the decree permitting the exiles to return to Judah[45] and subsequently furnished an alternative version of the edict.[46] Older historians[47] frequently argued that there was no evidence that Cyrus made a decree of this kind, or that he paid honour to the God of Israel. It is now clear from the Nabonidus Chronicle and the Cyrus cylinder that Cyrus was determined to exploit every opportunity for personal advancement, and one means of securing the good will of the various peoples in his empire was to restore the status of their captive gods[48] and proclaim a general amnesty for political prisoners in Babylonia. The second of the two decrees in Ezra, written in Aramaic, has been held by some scholars to be more reliable than the first, which is written in Hebrew. However, when compared with other ancient Near Eastern royal decrees, particularly those of the Persian period (*c.* 539-

331 B.C.), both documents appear to be substantially accurate and authentic.[49] The first was a characteristic royal proclamation framed for verbal utterance in the language of the people addressed,[50] while the second, a *dikrona* or official memorandum recording some decision for implementation, was not for public use but was reserved for the attention of the particular administrative official concerned, after which it was filed with other government documents. In this connection it is significant that the decree was found in the archives at Achmetha (Ecbatana),[51] where Cyrus is known to have stayed in his first regnal year (538 B.C.).

The returning exiles were led by descendants of the Davidic house, the most prominent of whom were Sheshbazzar[52] (from the Babylonian forms *Sin-ab-usur* or *Shamash-ab-usur*) and Zerubbabel[53] (the Babylonian *Zer-Babil*). Between 520 and 515 B.C., under the prophetic leadership of Haggai and Zechariah, the rebuilding of the Temple took place in Jerusalem. At this time a series of uprisings occurred in many parts of the Persian empire following the accession of Darius I (*c.* 522-486 B.C.), and in the expectation that the Persians might be overthrown and a Jewish state established Haggai[54] implied that Zerubbabel was the anointed one of God. When Darius finally triumphed the restored Davidic state failed to materialise, and Judah was governed internally by a high priest who was ultimately responsible to the governor appointed by the Persian court.

The recovery of official seal-impressions of the province of Judah during the fifth and fourth centuries B.C. have corroborated the semi-autonomous nature of this priestly commonwealth. Some of the impressions found on jar handles used the form *Yehud*, the official Aramaic designation of Judah, written in old Hebrew characters, whilst others depicted a later style of writing. One group of seals discovered at Tell en-Nasbeh, north of Jersualem, contained the puzzling abbreviation *msh*, the nature of which is obscure.[55] The existence of such seals and stamps implies a degree of local government which permitted the regulating of business life and the collecting of taxes. This is further borne out by the discovery of some fifth and fourth century B.C. coins with the word *Yehud* inscribed in Hebrew characters.[56] The references to the daric in Chronicles,[57] once considered anachronistic,[58] shows that the Attic drachma was used as a standard currency in Palestine from the fifth century B.C., replacing weighed amounts of silver and gold.

The chronology of the period in which Ezra and Nehemiah functioned presents certain difficulties, particularly in regard to the date when Ezra arrived in Jerusalem.[59] Some recent writers[60] have followed Albright in supposing that Ezra came to the capital in the thirty-seventh year of Artaxerxes I (428 B.C.) rather than in the seventh year (458 B.C.). It should be noted, however, that objections to the traditional view that Ezra arrived before Nehemiah in 458 B.C. are not as insuperable as Bright[61] would suppose. Travelling conditions in the days of Artaxerxes were not especially hazardous,[62] and when Ezra did arrive in Jerusalem it was his purpose to organise and regulate the religious affairs of the community, not to proclaim and enforce the provisions of a new legal code. After the reforms of 458 B.C. Ezra disappeared from the scene for some thirteen years, and it is not unreasonable to suppose that during this interval he was continuing his normal duties with the Persian central administration in Susa and Babylon. In his absence the abuses which he had sought to correct reappeared, and an attempt to build the city walls without approval[63] was halted by a royal decree[64] about 446 B.C.

If this was actually the case, the way would be open for Nehemiah to visit Jerusalem as civil governor in 445 B.C. with the purpose of rebuilding the city walls, remedying economic difficulties, and in company with Ezra promoting a religious revival based on the Law. The alleged failure of the early reforms of Ezra[65] reflects on the moral turpitude of the Jews rather than on the reforms themselves, a situation which occurred once more under Nehemiah in 433 B.C. Again, there is no mention of Ezra after the dedication of the city walls, about 445 B.C., suggesting that he may have died or returned to Babylonia. Furthermore, as Gordon has remarked, an impractical person such as Ezra would need the forceful administrative backing of Nehemiah to offset the mistakes and inadvertencies of an over-zealous approach to the contemporary social and religious scene.[66] Whilst no chronological reconstruction is completely free from difficulties, there seems no valid reason for rejecting the traditional position out of hand in favour of one which is equally beset with uncertainty.

From the records in Ezra and Nehemiah it is apparent that the development of the province of Judah met with considerable opposition, especially from the Samaritans, who apparently regarded Jerusalem as their rightful property. Under Nehemiah a climax was precipitated by a triumvirate consisting of Sanballat, governor of Samaria, Tobiah of Ammon and Geshem of Arabia.[67] Despite his name, Sanballat (Babylonian *Sin-uballit*) was almost certainly not a Babylonian, and the names of his sons, Deliah and Shelemiah, occurring in contemporary inscriptions from the Egyptian city of Elephantine,[68] are certainly Hebrew in form.

Two extra-Biblical sources attest to the position of Geshem at this time, one of which consisted of a collection of silver vessels found at Succoth (Tell el-Maskhutah) in Egypt. Three of the bowls bore Aramaic inscriptions containing north Arabic names, one of which read, "Qainu son of Geshem (Gusham) king of Qedar",[69] and was dated to the end of the fifth century B.C. The other inscription bearing the name of Geshem was recovered from Hegra in Arabia.[70] Taken together these sources indicate that Geshem ruled over a powerful Arab kingdom which included Sinai, part of the Nile delta, Edom, northern Arabia, and perhaps the southern part of Judah, where small altars similar to those from southern Arabia have been discovered.[71] This large Arab kingdom was under Persian control, with the local ruler functioning as a tributary.[72]

The family of Tobiah can be traced to the early second century B.C., as evidenced by the ruined family home at ᶜAraq el-Emir, north of the river Jabbok in Transjordan, which had been built in a splendid Hellenistic style between 200 and 175 B.C. by the last governor in the family. The name Tobiah is carved in Aramaic characters of the third century B.C. on the rock face near the ancestral tombs.[73] The Zeno papyri, discovered at Geraza in the Egyptian Fayyum, contained a letter from "Tobias the governor of Ammon", addressed to Zeno, an official in the government of Ptolemy Philadelphus (285-246 B.C.), stating that Tobias was dispatching a shipment of animals. The author of this letter was without doubt a descendant of the man who opposed Nehemiah.[74]

The genuine nature of the Aramaic correspondence in Ezra[75] has been amply demonstrated by the celebrated Elephantine papyri[76] discovered in 1903. These documents consisted of Aramaic letters written by Jews who were living in a military colony on the island of Elephantine near Assuan in Upper Egypt, and are dated within the period 500-400 B.C. At this time the fortress was known as Yeb, and the garrison derived a livelihood from trading, stone-quarrying, customs duties and other administrative functions. The Elephantine archives yielded a copy of a letter sent by the priests of the Jewish temple at Yeb to the governor of Judah, Bagoas, complaining that the temple had been destroyed in 410 B.C. as a result of Egyptian rivalry and requesting aid in rebuilding it. This document also said that the matter had been brought to the attention of the sons of Sanballat, governor of Samaria.

Other papyri consisted of legal contracts, deeds, agreements, official documents and private letters. All transactions were drawn up legally and attested by witnesses, sealed, and identified as to content by a notation on the exterior of the papyrus. The method was essentially Babylonian and was current in the Persian empire.[77] Marriage contracts were numerous, though the incidence of divorce documents was rare. Estate transactions were also prominent, and the texts showed that both men and women could engage in business. Exorbitant rates of interest were apparently charged on loans, and civil litigation often resulted. One papyrus contained the names of people who had donated gifts to the temple at Yeb, many of whom were women.[78]

The documents show that the Persian rulers took a genuine interest in the religious and social welfare of their subjects,[79] in addition to indicating the extent to which Aramaic had become the language of trade and diplomacy during the Persian period.[80] The papyri are important for the Book of Ezra because they show that the Aramaic used there was characteristic of the fifth century B.C., and that the letters in the fourth chapter exhibit the general language and style of that period.[81] There is some variation in the Biblical spelling of the royal names from that current after the fifth century B.C., and it is possible that the forms in Ezra were derived from earlier Persian renderings which were modified subsequently.

Some sidelights on the Persian regime have been furnished by discoveries which relate to the Book of Esther. The historicity of this composition has not as yet been vindicated by archaeology, although some who would dismiss the work as nothing more than an historical novel have been compelled to admit that the author was familiar with Persian administrative procedures, and knew of details connected with the construction of the royal palace at Susa (Shushan).[82] Excavations at the site from 1852 uncovered the hall and throne room of the palace on the north side of the mound. A trilingual inscription, written on the pedestals of four columns in the palace, gave a brief account of the way in which Artaxerxes II restored the building:

> "Says Artaxerxes, the great king, the king of kings . . . the son of king Darius, the son of king Darius Hystaspes: My ancestor Darius built this *apadana* (throne room of the palace) in former times. In the time of Artaxerxes, my grandfather, it was burnt by fire. I have restored it . . ."[83]

Further excavations under Marcel Dieulafoy from 1884 revealed that the ruined city had originally covered almost five thousand acres and was divided into four distinct areas comprising the citadel-mound, the royal city or "Shushan the palace",[84] the business and residential area or "Shushan the city", and the district on the plain to the west of the river. The royal palace included three courts of different sizes surrounded by halls and apartments. It was decorated with beautifully coloured glazed bricks on which figures of griffins, bulls and spearmen were executed in relief. The bulk of this type of decoration was from the time of Artaxerxes II[85]

Dieulafoy was able to throw light on the method employed by Haman for establishing a date on which the Jews would be destroyed[86] with the recovery of quadrangular dice on which were engraved the numbers one, two, five and six. The contemporary term for this prism was *pur*, from an Assyrian word *puru* meaning a "die" or "lot". Thus the explanation, "they cast Pur, that is, the lot" indicated that the Persian method of throwing dice was equivalent to the Jewish custom of "casting the lot".

The Persian empire collapsed under the onslaught of Alexander the Great about 332 B.C., and Mesopotamia experienced the full impact of Greek culture.[87] When Alexander died in 323 B.C. his empire was divided amongst his generals, and until 198 B.C. the Ptolemaic dynasty of Egypt controlled Palestine, after which it fell into the hands of the Seleucids. Under Antiochus Epiphanes IV (175-163 B.C.) a movement to bring Palestine into the full orbit of Hellenistic culture initiated the Maccabean revolt, which was followed by Roman control of the country in 63 B.C. Archaeological evidence for this period is rather scanty and is confined to a few sites. From inscriptions on some third century B.C. tombs at Marisa (Tell Sandaḥannah) it appears that the rise of Arab power in the fifth century B.C. forced the Edomites to migrate to Judaea, where they were known as Idumeans. The predominance of Greek names on the tomb walls, combined with the geometrical design of the city,[88] indicates the extent to which Hellenistic culture had progressed. At Samaria a number of Greek jar handles were recovered from third century B.C. levels, while at Bethel ten Ptolemaic coins from 285 B.C. to 182 B.C. were found, along with four coins from the time of Antiochus Epiphanes IV. At Shechem some coins from the first two Ptolemies testified to occupation from 312 B.C. to about 246 B.C.[89]

The Arab group which replaced the Edomites was itself succeeded by the Nabataeans, who were first mentioned historically as the object of an attack by Antigonus the Greek.[90] They established Petra as their capital where they carved out temples and homes in the red sandstone of the valley. They erected fortresses to guard strategic areas of their frontier, and established a distinctive culture which has become known through excavation of Nabataean sites.[91]

During the Greek period the religious community in Judaea reacted vigorously to the paganism of the surrounding nations. The scribes became established as the teachers of the Mosaic Law, and in the second century B.C. another separatist group, the Pharisees, arose to challenge the political and religious leadership of the Sadducees. The Samaritans flourished independently of the Jews at Shechem, and other religious groups broke away from the main stream of Judaism in an attempt to preserve the distinctive emphases of the Mosaic tradition. One of these communities which was established to the north-west of the Dead Sea has furnished the most important archaeological material of modern times, and this must now be surveyed briefly.

Chapter VII

THE DEAD SEA SCROLLS
AND THE OLD TESTAMENT

IN the early months of 1947 a Bedouin goatherd
named Muhammad Adh-Dhib of the Ta'amireh tribe
found a cave in the steep hillside rock of the Wadi
Qumran while searching for a lost goat. Throwing
a stone inside the cave with the intention of disturbing
any lurking animals, he heard instead a familiar sound
of something breaking. With the aid of a companion
he gained access to the cave where he discovered several
broken jars, some of which contained rolls of leather
and papyrus wrapped in cloth.[1] The tribesmen removed
these scrolls in the belief that they might have some
value as curios, and after an interval of some months
the documents were brought to the attention of the
Syrian Metropolitan of Jerusalem, Mar Athanasius Yeshue
Samuel. Realising their antiquity the Archbishop tried
to purchase all the manuscripts taken from the cave,
but in the end was only able to acquire five scrolls, one
of them a complete copy of Isaiah, and some other fragments.[2]

Shortly afterwards Professor E. L. Sukenik of the
Hebrew University of Jerusalem acquired several ancient
scrolls from a Bethlehem curio dealer. These were published posthumously in Jerusalem[3] and consisted of one
imperfect copy of Isaiah, a war document, and a hymnary
in several sections. The Isaiah manuscript was much more
fragmentary than that acquired by the Metropolitan,
although the prophecy from chapter forty onwards was
quite well preserved.

Ultimately the scrolls possessed by Archbishop Samuel

came to the attention of the American School of Oriental
Research in Jerusalem, and after J. C. Trever had
compared them with the archaic script of the Nash
papyrus[4] he became convinced of their antiquity and
photographed them without delay. A print of the Isaiah
scroll was sent to Professor W. F. Albright, who confirmed the remarkable nature of the material in the following
words:

> "My heartiest congratulations on the greatest manu-
> script discovery of modern times! There is no doubt
> in my mind that the script is more archaic than that
> of the Nash papyrus . . . there can happily be not the
> slightest doubt in the world about the genuineness
> of the manuscript . . ."[5]

The announcement of the discovery in the *Biblical
Archaeologist*[6] created a delicate situation for G. L.
Harding, who was in charge of archaeological discoveries
in Transjordan and Arab Palestine, because the artefacts
had been removed from Jordanian territory in contravention of the law. Since Harding was in complete ignorance
of the existence of the scrolls, the problem of redis-
covering and excavating the site was made very much more
difficult.

In 1949 the American Schools of Oriental Research
acquired temporary possession of the scrolls housed in
the Syrian Monastery of St. Mark in Jerusalem, and
three of them were published in facsimile in New Haven.[7]
The remaining scroll, thought to be the long-lost apocryphal
Book of Lamech,[8] defied all attempts at unrolling, and
it was only six years later that Professor J. Biberkraut
was able to determine the contents of the document.
It proved to be an Aramaic version of the early chapters
of Genesis dealing in paraphrase form with the times
of the Patriarchs, and was named *A Genesis Apocryphon*.[9]

The original cave at Qumran was located in 1949 and examined carefully by G. L. Harding, R. de Vaux, and members of the Dominican *École Biblique*. The task was all the more difficult because illicit investigators had anticipated the official party,[10] but despite this some six hundred fragments of papyri and leather were recovered, along with broken pottery and pieces of native linen. By this time the Bedouin tribesmen were aware of the value attaching to these artefacts, and they began an energetic search of the Qumran area in the hope of finding additional cave deposits. In 1951 further material was discovered at Wadi Murabba'at, eleven miles to the south of Qumran.[11] Coming from four caves it consisted of inscribed potsherds, fabric, Greek and Hebrew paypri, and on examination some of the latter were found to have been addressed to a certain Joshua ben Galgola by Simon Bar-Kokhba.[12]

The next year saw the exploration of other caves which yielded a great number of Biblical fragments, representing almost the entire Old Testament. From the third of the Qumran caves the archaeologists recovered two copper scrolls[13] which were so badly oxidised that it was impossible to unroll them. In 1956 they were specially treated and cut into strips at the Manchester College of Technology, with a textual loss of less than five per cent.[14] When translated they contained elaborate accounts of buried treasure in various locations.[15] Subsequent discoveries in the Khirbet Qumran and Khirbet Mird areas brought to eleven the number of caves in which manuscript deposits had been made. For convenience the archaeologists devised a system of enumeration which would relate the various caves to their corresponding localities. Thus 4Q represents the fourth cave at Qumran, while 2Mu signifies the second cave in the Wadi Murabba' at region.

In 1951 a party of archaeologists began to excavate

a ruined site or *khirbeh* on a shelf of rock near the Wadi
Qumran, which had been noticed by earlier visitors to the
area.[16] When properly uncovered the ruins constituted
the remains of a community building complete with
commodious natural reservoirs, and it was subsequently
linked with the manuscripts from 1Q by the discovery
of a jar identical with the remains of those found in
the first Qumran cave. As the digging progressed it
became apparent that the site had been occupied by a
religious community from about 110 B.C. to 31 B.C.,
after which an earthquake[17] damaged the buildings.
When a thirty-year interval had elapsed the site was
again inhabited by the sect until the buildings were
taken over by Roman soldiers in A.D. 68. It was used
for a short time by Jewish guerilla fighters during the
Second Jewish Revolt (A.D. 132-135), and subsequently
became derelict.

The community settlement[18] was dominated by a
defensive tower overlooking the principal building, a
structure some one hundred and twenty feet square.
A large room to the south was probably the main refectory,
adjoining which was a kitchen containing the remains
of hundreds of earthenware vessels. To the south-west
were a number of rooms which appeared to have been
used as assembly halls. In one of these were found
the ruins of plastered benches along each wall, while
in another the remains of inkwells, writing tables and
benches indicated the location of the community *scrip-
torium*, where the scrolls had been copied out by members
of the brotherhood.[19]

At the south-east corner of the site were the ruins of
a workshop whose facilities for smelting ore and baking
earthenware pointed to the self-supporting nature of
the community. Nearby were the cisterns and conduit
systems which supplied the settlement with an abundance
of water. Some of the cisterns were approached by means

of steps whose arrangement suggested that the pools were used periodically for baptismal rites.[20] When a room to the west of the main building was excavated in 1955, a cache of nearly six hundred coins was uncovered. They furnished an almost continuous occupational history of the site from about 139 B.C. to the time of the Second Jewish Revolt against Rome.[21] A further interesting feature of the site was the discovery of a burial ground adjacent to the *khirbeh*, in which the graves were laid out in parallel lines extending north and south. The skeletal remains subsequently recovered were in a poor state of preservation, and on examination[22] included some female bones. The simplicity of the graves and the absence of funerary ornamentation[23] testified to the austerity of the sect.

The nature of the literary interests and activities of the Qumran sectaries can be guaged from the scope of the manuscript discoveries. In addition to the Sukenik Isaiah scroll (1QISb),[24] the War document (1QM), the Thanksgiving Hymns (1QH), the Community Rule or Manual of Discipline (1QS), the St. Mark's Monastery Isaiah scroll (1QISa) and the Habakkuk Commentary (1QpHab), the sect possessed a number of extra-Biblical works as well as specifically apocryphal and pseudepigraphal writings. Of the canonical books only Esther is as yet unrepresented in the manuscript discoveries, which attest to the popularity of the Pentateuch, the prophetic writings, the Psalter and the Book of Daniel, of which numerous copies in varying degrees of completeness have survived.

The fact that several of the Qumran documents had been stored in jars reflected a long tradition of Near Eastern usage, where the jar was the equivalent of a private safe for valuables[25] or for the preservation of documents intended for posterity.[26] An apocryphal work described the steps taken to ensure the survival of literary material under these conditions as follows:

"Receive thou this writing that thou mayest know how to preserve the books which I shall deliver unto thee: and thou shalt set these in order and anoint them with oil of cedar and put them away in earthen vessels . . ."[27]

As a result of these precautions the large Isaiah scroll (1QISa) was in excellent condition when recovered and exhibited only ten lacunae and a number of minute holes, none of which presented any difficulties for the restoration of the text. On the other hand the Sukenik scroll (1QISb) had deteriorated badly with the passing of time, and when found was coated with a tacky layer of decayed leather which made restoration extremely difficult. The Habakkuk Commentary (1QpHab) was written in a clear hand, and as with some other scrolls the letters were suspended from faintly ruled lines. The text of this manuscript was divided up into columns, as was also the case with the Community Rule (1QS), which consisted of eleven columns of text with very few scribal corrections, and exhibited orthographic and philological features similar to those of the other texts.[28] The ink used in copying the manuscripts was a simple non-metallic compound.[29]

When the late Professor Sukenik reported that the scrolls in his possession were to be dated not later than A.D. 70, there were many scholars who found it hard to believe that the latest Hebrew manuscript sources (eighth to ninth centuries A.D.) could be antedated by almost a millennium. At once there arose a prolonged and acrimonious debate as to the authenticity and dating of the Qumran material[30] in which G. R. Driver of Oxford denied the early date assigned by Sukenik, Albright, Trever, Burrows and others on palaeographic grounds.[31] The chief protagonist in the United States was Solomon Zeitlin, the co-editor of the *Jewish Quarterly Review*, who adhered firmly to a medieval date for the scrolls and denounced their authenticity.[32] At the time the discussion commenced there was a lack of corroborating archaeological evidence from Qumran, which, however, has now been remedied as the result of subsequent discoveries and indicates that the scrolls emerged from a period commencing about 250 B.C. and terminating *c.* A.D. 68. Burrows assigned the earliest fragments from Qumran to about the third century B.C., and dated 1QISa and 1QS to *c.* 100 B.C. He held that the Habakkuk manuscript was written in the last quarter of the first century B.C.,[33] and assigned 1QM, 1QH and 1QISb along with the Genesis Apocryphon to the first half of the first century B.C. Carbon-14 dating of linen scraps from the first cave furnished an optimum range of 168 B.C. to A.D. 233,[34] the median of which confirmed the general dating of Albright,[35] Trever,[36] Birnbaum[37] and Sukenik,[38] arrived at after palaeographic study of the manuscript material.

The nature of the Qumran community (*yaḥad*) can be determined to a large extent from the scrolls themselves. In this connection the Community Rule (1QS) is the most important source, showing that the sect consisted of a group of priests and laymen living a communal life in strict dedication to God. The manuscript commenced with a statement of requirements from the person seeking to "enter into the Covenant",[39] and continued with the liturgical form of initiation.[40] Each member was required to renew his pledge of obedience annually,[41] at which time he was reminded of those deficiencies which would result in his expulsion from the brotherhood.[42] The fifth column of the text furnished the rules for community government,[43] and from these provisions it would appear that the sect was organised under the leadership of elders and priests to engage in constant Biblical study and to partake of a sacramental type of worship. The scroll makes it quite clear that the brother-hood regarded itself as the true Israel, awaiting the establishing of Divine rule upon earth. Their Hymns were either thanksgiving or benedictory compositions[44] which exhibited many points of contact with the Biblical Psalms. One thanksgiving hymn commenced as follows:

"I thank thee, Lord, for thou hast not forsaken me though I am living as a sojourner amongst alien people; (nor) hast thou judged me according to my iniquity . . . but thou hast rescued me from destruction . . ."[45]

The character of Biblical study indulged in by the sectaries is illustrated in part by the Habakkuk Commentary, in which portions of the Biblical text were followed by short allegorical or eschatological comments relating to the history of the brotherhood. This procedure was similar to that adopted in the ancient Jewish *midrashim*,[46] where cryptic references were reinforced by the division or abbreviation of words and the rearrangement of letters in a word. The Biblical text of the Commentary was followed by the term "pishro", meaning, "its interpretation is", after which came the scribal comments. Two short citations will illustrate the method adopted:

(Hab. 1:6) "*For behold, I raise up the Chaldeans* . . .
This interpretation refers to the Kittim, who are swift and formidable in battle, bent on the destruction of nations . . ."

(Hab. 1:13b) "*Wherefore lookest thou upon them that deal treacherously* . . .
This refers to the house of Absalom and their fellows who kept silent when accusations were brought against the righteous teacher,[47] and did not assist

him against the liar who rejected the Law in the presence of their entire assembly . . ."

The spiritual and temporal enemies of the sect were the wicked priest and the ruthless Kittim. The former opposed the righteous teacher, the leader of the brotherhood who expounded the Mosaic Law and communicated prophetic mysteries revealed to him by God.[48] The fact of his presence and activities at Qumran implied the near approach of the Messianic age. But apparently he was killed by the wicked priest,[49] perhaps by being delivered into the power of the Kittim, whom the sectaries envisaged apocalyptically as the agents of Divine wrath.

The identity of the Kittim has been a matter for considerable speculation. In Biblical Hebrew the name indicated Cyprus[50] or the general eastern Mediterranean region. Later Jewish authors used the term cryptically of any victorious power,[51] and as a result various scholars have identified them with the forces of Antiochus Epiphanes IV,[52] the Seleucid[53] or Roman[54] armies in the time of Alexander Janneus (103-76 B.C.), the military power of the Roman period proper,[55] some aggressive group functioning during the First Jewish War (A.D. 66-70),[56] or the Crusaders of the medieval Christian period.[57] A statement in the Commentary[58] that the Kittim sacrificed to their standards and worshipped their weapons might imply that they were to be identified with the Romans, who venerated their "eagles" and offered sacrifices to them.[59] If this assumption is correct the Commentary might well have envisaged the period culminating in the capture of Jerusalem under Pompey in 63 B.C. In the last analysis the identity of the individuals and groups mentioned in the Commentary must remain a matter for speculation until more conclusive evidence appears.

An important element in the thought of the sectaries was the expectation of the Messianic advent. The Community Rule required the brotherhood to live according to the Torah of Moses until the arrival of a prophet and two Messianic personages who were styled "the anointed ones of Aaron and Israel".[60] A manuscript found in 4Q consisted of a series of Biblical texts which summarised the Messianic concepts of the community,[61] while a document from the first cave entitled the *Rule of the Congregation*[62] described a banquet scene in the new Messianic age. It is interesting to note that the righteous teacher was never accorded Messianic status in the Qumran writings, but was always thought of as an interpreter of the Divine will and a herald of the Messianic period.

The identity of the Qumran sect became somewhat less problematical through the discovery of a mutilated manuscript in 4Q, which had affinity with an ancient Jewish work known as the Zadokite Document, dated between the tenth and twelfth centuries A.D., and first discovered in the *genizah*[63] of a Cairo synagogue in 1896.[64] A more correct designation of the Zadokite composition is the *Cairo Genizah Document of the Damascus Covenanters*, often shortened to the *Cairo Damascene Covenanters* (CDC). This literary work narrated the fortunes of a group of Jerusalem priests who were dispossessed during a reform movement. They migrated to Damascus and after assuming the title "Sons of Zadok" they formed the party of the New Covenant. As such they constituted a monastic sect within Judaism, and flourished under the leadership of one known as the "righteous teacher".

The fragments recovered from 4Q contained portions of CDC, and were supplemented by tattered manuscript pieces from 6Q.[65] This would indicate a close relationship between the sect of CDC and the Qumran brotherhood, and many scholars have regarded them as identical.[66] There can be no doubt as to the similarity existing between the linguistic forms of CDC and certain of the scrolls, as will be evident from the following citations:

CDC, V:6
"They who hold fast to him are for the life of eternity, and all the glory of man is for them . . ."

1QS, III:1 and IV:23
"He has not held them fast to Him who restores his life . . . and all the glory of man is for them."

CDC, IX:10B
". . . when the Messiah comes from Aaron and Israel . . ."

1QS, IX:11f.
"Until the advent of a Prophet and the anointed ones of Aaron and Israel . . ."

In both CDC and 1QS there is a reference to an unidentified work, the *Book of Hagu*, in which the Qumran sectaries were required to be instructed, and which may have been similar to or identical with[67] the Community Rule in part or in whole. If the Qumran brotherhood and the sect of CDC are identical, the migration to Damascus[68] may have taken place just before the beginning of the first century B.C.

Another contemporary religious movement with which the Qumran community has been identified by scholars is that of the Essenes,[69] about whom much was written in the early Christian period. Pliny[70] described one such community located near the Dead Sea, whilst Philo furnished considerable information about the Essenes themselves in his work *Quod Omnis Probus Sit Liber*[71] They apparently pursued a communal existence in isolated locations, working on the land and cultivating the arts of peace. Their piety was manifested not only in synagogue worship but also in the care which they exercised for each other. The Essenes abstained from marriage, a matter which Philo commented on in a later work,[72] on the ground that wives were jealous-minded creatures who could beguile and dominate a man at will. Another lengthy description of Essene life was furnished by Josephus,[73] who mentioned that one Essene sect indulged in the practice of marriage, not "out of regard to pleasure, but for the sake of posterity". In the *Antiquities* he gave a concise account of Essene life and doctrine, estimating that about four thousand men belonged to their monastic communities.[74] Hippolytus[75] described the moral and religious life of the Essenes and the various sects into which they were divided.

Another group which bore a superficial resemblance to the Qumran sect flourished in Egypt about 200 B.C. Known as the Therapeutae, their monastic life was described by Philo in a treatise entitled *On the Contemplative Life*.[76] They were recluses who devoted their energies to prayer, meditation and the study of their sacred writings, only assembling for community worship on the sabbath or on sacred seasons. This group admitted women to their fellowship, and as part of their religious exercises wrote commentaries and devotional poetry.

A cave-sect known as the Magharians was mentioned in the writings of Kirkisani, a tenth century A.D. Jewish sectary, who seems to have been influenced by some such source as the Zadokite Fragment.[77] He placed the Magharians in the pre-Christian era, and with this a Moslem historian Shahrastani (A.D. 1071-1153) agreed.[78] A Syriac letter from the Nestorian Patriarch of Seleucia to the Metropolitan of Elam mentioned the discovery of a rock-dwelling near Jericho about 800 A.D., which yielded several books.[79] Although it is attractive to suppose that this cave was one of those used by the Qumran sectaries, actual proof of a connection between the two groups is lacking.[80] Attempts have also been made to connect the Qumran brotherhood with the Ebionites of the first century A.D.,[81] and one writer[82] went so far as to identify the righteous teacher with Jesus Christ. However it must be remembered in this connection that the sectaries were essentially Jewish in outlook, whereas the Ebionites were Christian heretics.

Whilst there is a superficial resemblance between the Qumran community and the Essenes, there are certain very important differences. The Essenes were celibates who lived a communal existence and augmented their membership by accepting those who had renounced worldly life. While the Qumran sectaries were organised on a similar communal basis, they admitted women into their fellowship. In contrast with the Essenes, who did not indulge in animal sacrifices, the Qumran brotherhood allotted them a position of some significance.[83] Philo made it clear that the Essenes were pacifists by profession, whereas the War Scroll from Qumran,[84] even if interpreted in purely eschatological terms, demonstrates that the sectaries were far from being pacifists in intention. On these grounds alone there would seem to be reason for exercising a good deal of caution before making a positive identification of the Qumran fellowship with the Essenes, as the majority of scholars, following Milik, have done, a position for which there is no conclusive proof. The objections raised by del Medico, Zeitlin, Roth, Teicher and others would imply that if the sectaries are to be designated as Essenes at all, they can only be regarded as such in the most general sense.[85]

The discovery of the Qumran Biblical manuscripts

dispelled immediately the view held by many scholars concerning the improbability of recovering Hebrew manuscripts which antedated the formation of the Massoretic text.[86] With the antiquity of the scrolls now generally recognised, the palaeographers and textual critics have in their possession material which has advanced textual sources to an undreamed of extent. The Biblical manuscripts have confirmed the general opinion concerning the tremendous care exercised in the transmission of the Hebrew text, and have shown that much more respect must be accorded to the Massoretic or traditional text than has been the case in some quarters.[87] Early studies recognised that the scrolls followed Massoretic tradition more consistently than that of the Septuagint Greek,[88] and contained reflections of ancient sources in the matter of spelling and name-forms.[89] The orthography of the large Isaiah manuscript (1QISa) has certain phonetic characteristics which are less prominent in the Massoretic text, and which indicate some deviation from the tradition of the immediate pre-Christian period. It appears that this scroll furnished a contemporary phonetic spelling designed to facilitate reading without actually altering the time-honoured pronunciation, whereas the fragmentary Sukenik scroll (1QISb) followed the older form of spelling used prior to the destruction of the Second Temple.[90] Quite apart from their importance in reflecting the transitional phases of Hebrew orthography[91] the scrolls are of great value because they indicate the way in which Hebrew was pronounced just prior to the Christian era. Since no one can be absolutely certain as to how the various tongues of antiquity were enunciated, any information which contributes to the solution of this mystery is most welcome. By showing that Hebrew persisted in some areas as a living language despite the fact that most Palestinian Jews spoke Aramaic, the manuscripts have demonstrated the incorrectness of those views which maintained that Hebrew had become a dead language prior to the second century B.C.

Septuagint Greek textual studies have also received considerable stimulation from the discoveries at Qumran, particularly since fragments of 1 Samuel recovered from 4Q showed that the manuscript represented the same general tradition as that of the Hebrew text underlying the Septuagint version.[92] The divergences from both the Massoretic and Greek texts indicated that the fragments preserved a number of original readings which were not represented in the Massoretic and Greek traditions.[93] Such material is of great importance for the history of the Old Testament text since it points to a stage of development prior to the standardising of the literary tradition. From the evidence presented by the Qumran discoveries it appears that there were three distinct types of Biblical text in circulation amongst the Jews of the Second Commonwealth,[94] indicating that the Massoretic text was representative of only one body of literary tradition.[95]

While the Qumran Isaiah scrolls have failed to settle the long dispute as to the number of authors of that composition, they have shown that portions of the prophecy can no longer be assigned to the Maccabean period,[96] since the Book of Isaiah was in its present form not later than the beginning of the second century B.C. Similarly if the relationship existing between some fragments of Daniel found in 1Q[97] and the scrolls of Isaiah and Habakkuk is genuine, the commonly accepted Maccabean dating for Daniel[98] will need to be adjusted upwards.[99]

A number of readings from the large Isaiah scroll were incorporated into the Revised Standard Version rendering of Isaiah.[100] Probably the best of these was the correction of the A.V. of Isaiah 21:8, which spoke of a watchman who was observing the arrival of a messenger from the east suddenly introducing the meaningless figure of a wild beast,

"And he cried, A lion: My lord, I stand continually upon the watchtower . . ."

which when corrected by reference to the St. Mark's Isaiah manuscript read,

"Then he who saw cried: Upon a watchtower I stand . . ."

Another reading preserved by both Isaiah scrolls but ignored by the R.S.V. is worthy of mention. The Massoretic text of Isaiah 53:11, as rendered by the A.V. and R.V. reads,

"He shall see of the travail of his soul and shall be satisfied . . ."

The Septuagint Greek inserted the word "light" before the second verb of the sentence, and this was confirmed independently by the Qumran versions. Thus the passage should read,

"After the travail of his soul he will see light, he will be satisfied . . ."

The majority of divergences from the traditional text exhibited by the Habakkuk Commentary comprise mostly errors of transcription, dictation or spelling. Perhaps one reading which may be superior to the Massoretic text is in Habakkuk 1:11, where the scroll reads, ". . . and he made his might his god" instead of the traditional "guilty man whose might is his god". Another variant occurs in Habakkuk 2:16, where the Massoretic reading for "be uncircumcised" has been altered in the scroll to "stagger", involving a minor change in the order of

PLATE 11. *The large Isaiah Scroll.* Approximately 1000 years older than the earliest manuscript of Isaiah previously known, the scroll is open at Chapter 35:9 to 40:28.

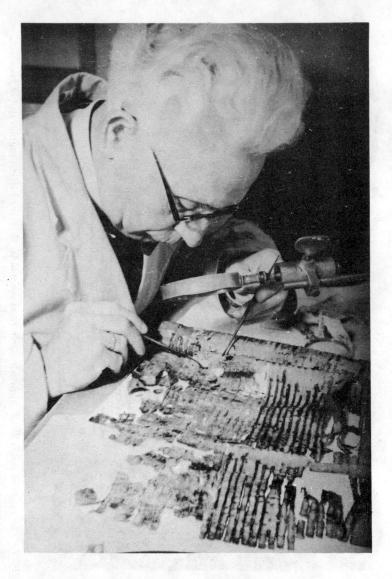

PLATE 12. Restoring the Genesis Apocryphon.
Mr. James Biberkraut is at work piecing together the various
fragments of the scroll. The difficulty of the task and the great skill
required for successful completion is immediately apparent.

the consonants. The substitution of "his sword" in the Commentary for "his net" in the Massoretic text of Habakkuk 1:17 produces a more intelligible rendering: "Therefore he bares his sword, slaying nations for ever without pity." From these and other variants it would appear that the Commentary has preserved a popular form of the Massoretic text.

That the Qumran manuscripts have had a greater importance for the Biblical text[101] than the canon is now apparent after fifteen years of study, and much more light can be expected to be thrown upon such versions as the Samaritan Pentateuch and the Septuagint in the future. A brief survey such as this can do no more than begin to hint at the revolutionary importance of the scrolls for large areas of Biblical study, a fact which is attested by the enormous literary output on the subject to date. This will undoubtedly increase as time goes on and as further manuscripts and artefacts are recovered from the Qumran area. Together with extant material it will do much to extend the frontiers of knowledge in the areas of history, religion and sacred literature.

There can be no doubt that the scrolls have ushered in a new era of Biblical study in which much that was known will be confirmed, and much that was accepted as fact will need to be revised. Not the least benefit will be a movement towards the ultimate reconstruction of a genuine pre-Christian Old Testament text,[102] making the ancient Word of God more intelligible for its modern readers.

NOTES TO CHAPTERS

CHAPTER I

1. This ancient Babylonian word is still used in modern Arabic and means "elevated". The plural form of *tell* is *tulul*. References to both inhabited and ruined sites occur in Josh. 8:28.; 11:13. In the former the A.V. rendered the Hebrew *tēl* by "heap" (R.S.V. "heap of ruins"); in the latter the plural word *tillām* (R.S.V. "mounds") by "strength".

2. E. Chiera, *They Wrote on Clay* (1939), p. 34f., has illustrated the various layers of a mound by reference to typical artefacts of the different occupational levels. For the general procedure followed by excavators cf. *WMTS*, p. 10 seq.

3. The archaeologist is faced with special problems when mounds have modern settlements located on or around them. Cf. *LAP*, p. 5.

4. Nothing is known about the origin of irrigation. Cf. *BCNE*, pp. 31 ff.

5. S. Lloyd and F. Safar, *JNES* (1945), IV, pp. 255 seq.; *CAEM*, p. 1 seq.

6. M. E. L. Mallowan, *Annals of Archaeology and Anthropology, University of Liverpool* (1933), XX, p. 127 seq.; *Proceedings of the First International Congress of Prehistoric and Protohistoric Sciences* (1932; 1934), pp. 165 ff.

7. E. A. Speiser, *Asia* (1938), XXXVIII, p. 543; *BASOR* (1937), No. 66, p.18; *ibid.* (1938), No. 70, p. 6 f.

8. *AP*, p. 47.

9. M. von Oppenheim, *Der Tel Halaf, eine neue Kultur im ältesten Mesopotamien* (1931); *CAEM*, p. 16 seq.

10. *FSAC*, p. 92.

11. For kilns of this type recovered from Carchemish and Tepe Gawra cf. E. A. Spieser, *BASOR* (1937), No. 66, p. 15 f.

12. *FSAC*, p. 90; *LAP*, p. 15 and pl. 1.

13. *NLMAE*, p. 113 seq.; *CAEM*, p. 73 seq.

14. H. R. Hall and C. L. Woolley, *Ur Excavations: I, Al-'Ubaid* (1927).

15. *LAP*, p. 17.

16. E. A. Speiser, *BASOR* (1937) No. 65, p. 8.; *ibid.* (1937) No. 66, p. 3 seq.; *CAEM*, pp. 46 seq., 162 seq.

17. For the influence of this method of construction upon Egyptian architecture, cf. *BCNE*, p. 126 seq.

18. J. Jordan, *Uruk-Warka nach den Ausgrabungen durch die Deutsche Orient-gesellschaft* (1920); *CAEM*, p. 97 seq.

19. *CAEM*, p. 110 seq. The term is related to the Assyrian *ziqquratu*, "a mountain top". The *ziggurat* was an artificial mound on which a shrine was erected, but the word is often used to include the structure also.

20. *BCNE*, p. 55.

21. In his comments on the antiquity of property markings D. Diringer (*The Story of the Aleph Beth*, 1960, p. 22) omits any reference to predynastic Mesopotamian practices.

22. A seal from the Uruk period is figured in *LAP*, pl. 4.

23. Cf. A. Falkenstein, *Archaische Texte aus Uruk* (1940), pp. 49, 62; *FSAC*, p. 146.

24. *CAEM*, pp. 106 f.; 143 seq.

25. *FSAC*, p. 145.

26. T. Jacobsen in H. Frankfort (Ed.), *Before Philosophy* (1949), p. 140 f., regards this as the characteristic feature of Mesopotamian agriculture.

27. The transition from prehistory to historical cultural forms in Mesopotamia is sometimes designated as "urban revolution", as in V. G. Childe, *What Happened in History* (1950), p. 89 seq. Frankfort, *BCNE*, p. 61, accuses Childe of applying inappropriate categories to ancient Near Eastern cultural developments to produce a "Marxist slant". The term "urban revolution" is rather unfortunate, since it does not apply to ancient Egyptian cultural trends, as might otherwise be expected.

28. *BCNE*, p. 58 f.

29. *BCNE*, p. 66.

30. *BCNE*, p. 67.

31. A Sumerian word meaning "great man", usually translated "king".

32. Cf. H. Frankfort, *Kingship and the Gods* (1948), p. 237 f.

33. S. Langdon, *Oxford Editions of Cuneiform Texts* (1923), II, Bk. 1-4, p. 8 seq.; cf. G. A. Barton, *The Royal Inscriptions of Sumer and Akkad* (1929), p. 346 seq.; *ANET*, p. 265 f.

34. *TS*, p. 21. Berossus of Babylon (third century B.C.) extended the list to ten and increased the length of their reigns. How far there is a connection between this tradition and the ten patriarchs which existed from Adam to Moses is difficult to estimate. Cf. *AB*, p. 320.

35. S. Langdon, *Semitic Mythology* (1931), p. 206.

36. A. Heidel, *The Gilgamesh Epic and Old Testament Parallels* (1949 ed.), p. 103 f.

37. The sun-deity.

38. S. N. Kramer, *Sumerian Mythology* (1944), p. 97 f.

39. Originally thought to be in south-western Iran (*BASOR*, 1944, No. 96, p. 18 seq.), Dilmun is now identified with the small desert island of Bahrein in the Persian Gulf, where excavations took place from 1953 under P. V. Glob of Denmark.

The structure of the ruined temples and the design of other artefacts showed close affinity with the predynastic and early dynastic periods of Mesopotamia and with the Indus civilisation. Ancient Bahrein was a focal point of maritime trade between Mesopotamia and India, and was the home of rich merchants, presumably the *alik Dilmun* ("the travellers to Dilmun") of the Ur tablets. Cf. *Illustrated London News* (Jan. 4, 1958), p. 14 ff.; *ibid* (Jan. 11, 1958), p. 54 f.

40. E. F. Smith, *The Museum Journal* (1931), XXII, p. 200 f.

41. L. C. Watelin and S. Langdon, *Excavations at Kish IV*, 1925-30 (1934), p. 40 seq.; *LAP*, pl. 8.

42. S. Langdon, *JRAS* (1930), p. 603.

43. *UC*, p. 21 seq.; *Antiquaries Journal* (1930), X, p. 329 seq.

44. A. Parrot, *The Flood and Noah's Ark* (1955), p. 50 seq.

45. As Parrot has shown (*Tello*, 1948, p. 58), a sterile deposit need not be alluvial in origin, but could constitute a sub-foundation of packed soil.

46. In view of the difficulties involved, the enthusiastic pronouncements of men such as Sir Charles Marston, *The Bible is True* (1934), p. 67, that Woolley and Langdon had simultaneously discovered the Noachian Flood deposits are to be deplored.

47. J. Bright, *BA* (1942), V, No. 4, p. 58.

48. Cf. Gen. 7:11. Watelin (*Kish IV*, 1934, p. 43) found no trace of marine organisms in the alluvial layers at Ur and Kish.

49. Watelin, *Kish IV*, pp. 40 ff.

50. A. Parrot, *The Flood and Noah's Ark*, p. 55 f. He depicts ancient Mesopotamian vessels in pl. 6 and 7.

51. Some of these are humorously described by Parrot, *The Flood and Noah's Ark*, p. 63 seq.

52. For the theory of carbon-14 dating *vide* W. F. Libby, *Radiocarbon Dating* (1954).

53. Cf. *LAP*, p. 31.

54. *UC*, p. 73; cf. *LAP*. p. 33.

55. *UC*, pp. 74 ff.

56. For the view that these tombs were the repository of priests and priestesses sacrificed in fertility rites, and not royal persons, cf. S. Smith, *JRAS* (1928), p. 862 seq.; Cp. H. Frankfort, *ibid.* (1937), p. 341 f.; E. A. Speiser, *Antiquity* (1934), VII, p. 451.; H. Frankfort, *Kingship and the Gods* (1948), p. 400 n 12.

57. *LAP*, pl. 12.

58. *UC*, p. 39 seq. Woolley dated the cemetery *c.* 3500-3200 B.C. (*UR Excavations II, The Royal Cemetery* (1934), p. 223), but this has been criticised amongst others by Frankfort, *JRAS* (1937), p. 332 seq. Albright has suggested a date of *c.* 2500 B.C. Cf. *BASOR* (1942), No. 88, p. 32.; *AJA* (1943) XLVII, p. 492.

59. *UC*, pl. 5 (*a*); 6.

60. *TS*, pl. 9; *UC*, p. 59 f.

61. *TS*, pl. 14 and p. 50 seq.

62. *WBA*, p. 34.

63. R. F. S. Starr, *Nuzi, Report on the Excavations at Yorgan Tepa near Kirkuk, Iraq* (1939), I, p. 23.

64. *LAP*, pl. 17.

65. *FSAC*, p. 191.

66. *UC*, p. 89 seq.; *TS*, p. 141 seq., pl. 23 and 24. Cf. *Ur Excavations V, The Ziggurat and Its Surroundings* (1939).

67. *UC*, p. 93 f. Cf. pl. 9 (*b*).

68. *LAP*, pl. 20.

69. *UC*, pl. 10 (*a*). Cf. C. L. Woolley, *The Development of Sumerian Art* (1935), p. 112. This is the earliest representation of an angel so far discovered.

70. *LAP*, p. 44.

71. *TS*, p. 169. Cf. S. N. Kramer, *Lamentation Over the Destruction of Ur. Assyriological Studies, Oriental Institute* (1940), XII, p. 56 f.

72. Cf. A. Parrot, *Babylon and the Old Testament* (1958), p. 68 seq.

73. *LAP*, pp. 48 ff. and pl. 22. It is now in the Louvre in Paris.

74. *ANET*, p. 164 seq.; *ANE*, p. 138 seq. Portions of the *stele* were mutilated by the Elamites, but the damaged sections have survived for the most part in other copies of the Code.

75. "The year he enacted the law of the land". The extant *stele* is a copy of the original, since the prologue refers to events which occurred much later than the second year of his rule.

76. E.g., S. A. Cook, *The Laws of Moses and the Code of Hammurabi* (1903); W. W. Davies, *The Codes of Hammurabi and Moses* (1905).

77. Cf. R. C. Thompson, *Assyrian Medical Texts* (1923); *ibid. The Assyrian Herbal* (1924); *id. A Dictionary of Assyrian Chemistry and Geology* (1936).

78. O. Neugebauer, *Mathematische Keilschrift-Texte* (1935-37), I-III.

79. *BG*, p. 8.

80. *BG*, p. 40 f.

81. *BG*, p. 44.

82. Heidel (*BG*, p. 139) has stressed that the relationship between the Hebrew and Babylonian accounts is still very much of an open question.

83. *ANET*, p. 72 seq.; *ANE*, p. 40 seq.

84. A. Heidel, *The Gilgamesh Epic and Old Testament Parallels* (1949), p. 85 f.

85. Gen. 14:6, *et. al.*

86. For the earlier cuneiform texts *vide* R. H. Pfeiffer and E. A. Speiser, *AASOR* (1935-36), XVI; E. Chiera, *Joint Expedition with the Iraq Museum at Nuzi* (1927-39),

I-VI; *Harvard Semitic Series* (1929), V; *ibid.* (1932), IX; *id.* (1942), XII.

87. Also known as Hapiri in cuneiform texts, which may be the same as the 'Aperu or 'Apiru of such Egyptian inscriptions as the *stele* of Sethi I (*c.* 1319-1300 B.C.). Cf. W. F. Albright, *AASOR* (1926), VI, p. 35 f.; A. Rowe, *The Topography and History of Beth-Shan* (1930), p. 29 f. For an examination of the problems connected with the origin and nature of the Habiru cf. M. Greenberg, *The Hab/piru* (1955), p. 3 seq.

88. W. F. Albright, *The Archaeology of Palestine and the Bible* (1935), p. 206 f.; cf. *FSAC*, p. 240.

CHAPTER II

1. Cf. *TS*, p. 140 seq.; *UC*, p. 87 seq.
2. *TJ*, I, p. 4.
3. Cf. the early reports in *Syria, Revue d'Art orientale et d'archéologie* (1935), XVI, pp. 1 seq., 117 seq.; *ibid* (1936), XVII, p. 1 seq.; *id.* (1937), XVIII p. 54 seq.
4. *BA* (1948), XI, No. 1, p. 5.
5. *WBA*, p. 36 f. and pl. 11.
6. *BA* (1948), XI, No. 1, p. 8 f and pl. 5.
7. A. Parrot, *Mari une ville perdue* (1935), p. 161.
8. *BA* (1948), XI, No. 1, p. 13.
9. *FSAC*, p. 236 f.; *JBL* (1924), XLIII, p. 385 seq.
10. *FSAC*, p. 237 f.; *WBA*, p. 42.
11. Gen. 49:29. Cf. Judg. 20:16., 1 Chron. 12:2.
12. *BA* (1948), XI, No. 1, p. 16 f.
13. C. H. Gordon, *The Living Past* (1941), p. 156 seq.; *IOTT*, p. 100 seq.
14. R. H. Pfeiffer and E. A. Speiser, *AASOR* (1936),

XVI, pp. 59 ff. For even earlier evidence of primitive democratic institutions cf. T. Jacobsen, *JNES* (1943), II, No. 3, p. 159 seq.

15. The "teraphim" of Genesis 31:19 *et al.*
16. *BA* (1940), III, No. 1, p. 6.
17. *BA* (1940), III, No. 1, p. 3.
18. *BA* (1940), III, No. 1, p. 5.
19. Gen. 15:2 f. Cf. *CBQ* (1944), VI, p. 391 seq.
20. Gen. 16:2. Two generations later Rachel gave Bilhah to Jacob (Gen. 30:3) in conformity with the same custom.
21. Gen. 21:11.
22. *ANET*, p. 159 f.
23. Gen. 25:31 seq.
24. *BA* (1940), III, No. 1, p. 5.
25. Gen. 31-43.
26. Gen. 31:41.
27. Gen. 31:19.
28. Gen. 31:15. In Nuzu society "foreign women" were usually slaves occupying an inferior position in the household.
29. Gen. 27:27 seq.; 49:3 seq.
30. Cf. Gen. 27:33.
31. *BA* (1940), III, No. 1, p. 8.
32. E.g., *WBA*, p. 40., *BHI*, p. 72 f.; cf. *FSAC*, p. 164 f.
33. D. J. Wiseman and A. Goetze, *Journal of Cuneiform Studies* (1959), XIII, pp. 29, 37.
34. A. Parrot, *Syria, Revue d'Art orientale et d'archéologie* (1955), XXXII, p. 323.
35. P. Montet, *Byblos et l'Egypte* (1928), p. 91, pl. 52. Albright objected that it had no hump and therefore was not a camel (*JBL*, 1945, LXIV, p. 288), but as R. de Vaux pointed out (*RB* 1949, LVI, p. 9 n 4 f.) there is a socket in the back to which the hump and its load had been attached separately.
36. The Tell Halaf sculptured relief (*LAP*, p. 55 and

pl. 25) is thus far from being "one of the earliest known representations of the camel".

37. *FSAC*, p. 237; cf. H. H. Rowley in *BJRL* (1949), XXXIII, p. 76.

38. The places visited by Abraham lie in a zone whose annual rainfall is between ten and twenty inches, which is suited to the requirements of sheep. Cf. *BA* (1955), XVIII, No. 1, p. 4.

39. *WHAB*, p. 23.

40. *WBA*, p. 46.

41. Cf. Gen. 13:18, 26:23, 28:10; 33:18, 35:1, 37:17.

42. N. Glueck, *The Other Side of the Jordan* (1940), p. 114 seq.; *ibid. BA* (1955) XVIII, No. 1, p. 2 seq.; *WMTS*, p. 71.

43. Num. 13:22, *i.e., c.* 1725 B.C. The original name of Hebron may have been Kiriath-arba (Gen. 23:2, 35:27), hence the explanatory gloss of Gen. 13:18.

44. *TJ*, I, p. 5.

45. *ANET*, p. 18 seq.

46. Probably the "east" of Gen. 29:1.

47. Deut. 8:8.

48. *ARE*, I, Sect. 496; cf. *ANET*, p. 19 f., *LAP*, p. 82.

49. Gen. 19:1 seq.

50. W. F. Albright, *The Archaeology of Palestine and the Bible* (1935), pp. 133 ff.

51. R. A. S. Macalister, *The Excavation of Gezer* (1912), 3 Vols.

52. G. Schumacher and C. Steuernagel, *Tell El-Mutesellim* (1908).

53. Cf. G. Loud, *The Megiddo Ivories* (1939); *ANET*, p. 263; *ANE*, p. 187.

54. Gen. 23:3 seq.

55. Gen. 23:9.

56. Gen. 23:11.

57. Gen. 23:17.

58. M. R. Lehmann, *BASOR* (1953), No. 129, p. 15 seq.

59. E.g. *BHI*, p. 73.

60. *Orientalia* (1950), XIX, p. 509.

61. C. F. A. Schaeffer, *Ugaritica I* (1939), pp. 54 ff.

62. Y. Yadin, *Hazor II* (1960), p. 86.

63. R. W. Ehrich (Ed.) *Relative Chronologies in Old World Archaeology* (1954), p. 10 seq.

64. *IOTT*, p. 108.

65. *BA* (1948), XI, No. 1, p. 18; cf. *BASOR* (1954), No. 133, p. 26 seq.; M. Noth *Gesammelte Studien zum Alten Testament* (1957), p. 142 seq.

66. Josh. 24:32, Judg. 9:4.

67. G. F. Owen, *Archaeology and the Bible* (1961), p. 120.

CHAPTER III

1. V. G. Childe, *New Light From the Most Ancient East* (1953 ed.), p. 33 f.

2. G. Brunton and G. Caton-Thompson, *The Badarian Civilisation* (1928), p. 19 seq.

3. V. G. Childe, *New Light From the Most Ancient East*, p. 56 seq.

4. The Palermo Stone (cf. *LAP*, pp. 70, 74 and pl. 27), which recorded the succession of pharoahs from the first dynasty, had the union of the Two Lands (Upper and Lower Egypt) as its theme.

5. R. Dussaud, Syria, *Revue d'Art orientale et d'archéologie* (1935), XVI, p. 320 seq.; H. Frankfort, *Cylinder Seals* (1939), p. 292 seq.; A Scharff, *Zeitschrift für ägyptische Sprache und Altestumskunde* (1935), LXXI, p. 89 seq.; H. Frankfort, *American Journal of Semitic Languages and Literatures* (1941), LVIII, p. 329 seq.; H. J. Kantor, *JNES* (1944), III, p. 110 seq.

6. I. E. S. Edwards, *The Pyramids of Egypt* (1947), p. 85 seq.

7. The Beni-Hasan tableau belongs to this period. Cf. P. E. Newberry, *Beni-Hasan I* (1893), pl. 30.

8. The origin of the Hyksos is problematical. Cf. H. Stock, *Studien zur Geschichte und Archäologie der 13 bis 17 Dynastie Ägyptens* (1942), p. 19 seq.; R. M. Engberg, *The Hyksos Reconsidered* (1939), p. 4 seq.; T. Säve-Söderberg, *JEA* (1951), XXXVII, p. 53 seq.

9. An Egyptian priest who lived under Ptolemy II Philadelphus (285-246 B.C.). Manetho interpreted "Hyksos" as "shepherd-kings", from two Egyptian words. For a more correct etymology cf. A Erman and H. Grapow, *Wörterbuch der ägyptischen Sprache* (1929), III, p. 171. In the Execration Texts of *c.* 1960 B.C. (*ANET*, p. 328 f.) they were known as *hekau khasut*.

10. In Josephus, *Contra Apion*, i. 14.

11. Cf. W. F. Albright in P. W. Long (Ed.) *Studies in the History of Culture* (1942) pp. 21 ff.

12. *FSAC*, p. 206.

13. Identified with San el-Hagar, and known successively as Avaris (before 1500 B.C.), "Houses of Rameses" (*c.* 1300-1100 B.C.), Tanis (after 1100 B.C.), and Zoan (Num. 13:22).

14. *WMTS*, p. 72.

15. Num. 13:22.

16. This view assumes that Rameses was a rebuilt and expanded Avaris, and is not to be identified with Qantir, a few miles to the south.

17. Lengthened to four hundred and thirty years in Exod. 12:40.

18. H. M. Orlinsky, *Ancient Israel* (1954), p. 33 f.

19. Avaris was also the capital of the Nineteenth Dynasty rulers after 1300 B.C.

20. Gen. 47:13 seq. Cf. G. Steindorf and K. C. Seele, *When Egypt Ruled the East* (1942), p. 88.

21. H. H. Rowley, *From Joseph to Joshua* (1950), pp. 72 f.,

78; Gordon, *IOTT*, p. 103 f, have dated the Patriarchs some centuries after the early second millennium B.C. on the ground that there were only three generations between the Patriarchal period and the conquest of Canaan. However, the genealogical tables on which their argument is based have not preserved precise and complete information regarding ancestry before the conquest, but merely the general designation of clan and tribe. Cf. *WBA*, p. 50 n 5.

22. Gen. 39:4.
23. Gen. 41:40.
24. Gen. 45:8.
25. *WBA*. p. 53.
26. Gen. 40:2.
27. Gen. 40:20.
28. Gen. 41:8.
29. Gen. 46:34. Cf. Gen. 43:32.
30. Gen. 50:22. Cf. Josh. 24:29; Judg. 2:8.
31. Gen. 50:2, 26.
32. J. A. Thompson, *Archaeology and the Old Testament* (1959), p. 37 f.
33. This is the correct meaning of "bow the knee" in the A.V. of Gen. 41:43.
34. Cf. Exod. 1:14, 5:16; *ARE*, II, Sect. 758 f.
35. S. L. Caiger, *Bible and Spade* (1936), p. 61.
36. S. L. Caiger, *Bible and Spade*, p. 62.
37. Gen. 39:7 seq.
38. *ANET*, p. 24; *ANE*, p. 12. The story was intended primarily for entertainment, not for moral instruction or guidance.
39. J. A. Wilson, *The Burden of Egypt* (1951), p. 155 seq. The Eighteenth Dynasty queen Hatshepsut recorded her attempts in this direction: "I have restored that which was ruins, I have raised up that which was unfinished, since the Asiatics were in the midst of Avaris of the Northland, and the barbarians were in the midst of them". *ARE*, II, Sect. 303.

40. P. Montet, *Les nouvelles fouilles de Tanis* (1929-33).

41. Exod. 1:11. Contemporary Egyptian texts mention that some Apiru were employed to drag the stones used in temple construction, probably at these sites.

42. At Pithom, as at other sites near Luxor in the Nineteenth and Twentieth Dynasties, use was made of "bricks without straw", *i.e.*, having a finely-chopped stubble content rather than the more bulky straw from the threshing floor. The organic compounds produced by decaying vegetable matter increased the strength and plasticity of the clay threefold. Cf. J. Alexander, *Colloid Chemistry: Principles and Applications* (1937), p. 199; *BA* (1950), XIII, No. 2, p. 24 seq.

43. *WBA*, p. 59. The entire area became known as the "land of Rameses". Cf. Gen. 47:11.

44. For a review of the various theories cf. H. H. Rowley in *BJRL* (1938), XXII, p. 243 seq.

45. J. Garstang, *Joshua-Judges* (1931), p. 146; *ibid.* *The Story of Jericho* (1940), p. 157 seq.

46. Cf. *BA* (1960), XXIII, No. 1, p. 2 seq.

47. G. L. Robinson, *The Bearing of Archaeology on the Old Testament* (1941), p. 58. Cf. *ANET*, p. 262 seq.; *LAP*, pp. 98 ff.

48. H. R. Hall, *Ancient History of the Near East* (1926), p. 409.

49. 1 Kings 6:1.

50. Cf. *IOTT*, pp. 104 n 6, 294 f.

51. J. W. Jack, *The Date of the Exodus* (1925), p. 200 seq.

52. P. Montet, *Le Drame d'Avaris* (1940), p. 18 seq.; *WHAB*, p. 37.

53. N. Glueck, *The Other Side of the Jordan* (1940), p. 125 seq. Albright in H. H. Rowley (Ed.) *The Old Testament and Modern Study* (1951), p. 4, has stated that certain details of the findings may need to be modified.

54. S. L. Caiger, *Bible and Spade*, p. 111 f.; *ANET*, p. 378.

55. This may be a scribal error, however, since the *stele* contains other transcriptional mistakes.

56. Obviously the fugitives could not have taken this route, as earlier scholars used to claim. For a tentative map of the journey *vide WHAB*, p. 41.

57. Exod. 13:18.

58. Exod. 14.

59. *OTC*, p. 142.

60. Exod. 15:27; Num. 33:9.

61. Num. 33:12.

62. Exod. 17:1; Num. 33:14.

63. *FSAC*, p. 257; cf. *ANET*, p. 229.

64. Num. 33:5 seq.

65. Exod. 24:3 seq.

66. Exod. 26-27, 35-38.

67. *BA* (1947), X, No. 3, pp. 55, 60 f. The Canaanite deity El may also have had some such portable shrine. Cf. *BASOR* (1943), No. 91, p. 39 seq.

68. J. Morgenstern, *Hebrew Union College Annual* (1928), V, p. 81 seq.; *ibid.* (1942-3), XVII, p. 153 seq.; *id.* (1943-4), XVIII, p. 1 seq.

69. *FSAC*, p. 266.

70. F. R. Steele, *American Journal of Archaeology* (1948), LII, p. 425 seq. and pls. XXXIX-XLV; *ANET*, pp. 159 ff.

71. A. Goetze, *Sumer* (1948), IV, p. 63 seq. and pls. I-IV; P. A. Pohl, *Orientalia* (1949), XVIII, p. 126 seq. and pls X-XX; *ANET*, pp. 161 ff.; *ANE*, p. 133 seq.

72. Concerning the division of oxen after fatal combat. Cf. Exod. 21:35.

73. *TH*, p. 91. The Code is translated in *ANET*, p. 188 seq.

74. *TH*, p. 95. For a comparative study *vide* E. Cuq,

Études sur le droit babylonien, les lois assyriennes et les lois hittites (1929); J. M. P. Smith, *The Origin and History of Hebrew Law* (1931); T. J. Meek, *Hebrew Origins* (1950), p. 49 seq.; *AB*, p. 378 seq.

75. Deut. 24:1.

76. Code of Hammurabi, Sect. 142. Considerations of space prevent a more detailed comparison of Mosaic and other Near Eastern laws. As A. Jeremias long ago indicated (*The Old Testament in the Light of the Ancient Near East*, 1911, II, p. 112), there are far-reaching differences which are ultimately theological rather than sociological in origin. The form of many Pentateuchal legal passages suggests a second millennium B.C. cultural milieu, whilst in the opinion of the author the medical sections of Leviticus are unique to the Israelites, and are to be dated specifically in the Mosaic period.

77. *BA* (1954), XVII, No. 3, p. 50 seq., reprinted in G. E. Mendenhall, *Law and Covenant in Israel and the Ancient Near East* (1955).

78. Cf. Exod. 20:1 f.; Josh. 24:2.

79. Cf. Exod. 20:2; Josh. 24:2 f.

80. Cf. *ANET*, p. 204; Deut. 7:7.

81. Cf. Exod. 20:3, 34:14; Josh. 24:14.

82. Cf. Exod. 25:16, 21; Deut. 31:9 seq.; Josh. 24:26; 1 Kings 8:9.

83. In Joshua 24:22 the Israelites replace the heathen gods as witnesses. But cf. Isa. 1:2; Hos. 2:21 f.; Micah 6:2.

84. Cf. the hortatory injunctions of Exod. 23:20 seq.; Lev. 26:3 seq.; Deut. 27:12 seq.

CHAPTER IV

1. *LAP*, p. 131.

2. Num. 20:14 seq.
3. N. Glueck, *The Other Side of the Jordan*, p. 128 f.
4. Num. 22-24. The *baru* or diviner commonly functioned as a staff adviser attached to military forces.
5. *WBA*, p. 74.
6. E.g. S. H. Hooke in H. W. Robinson (Ed.), *Record and Revelation* (1938), p. 359.
7. *WBA*, p. 75. For the name "Canaan" cf. *BASOR* (1946), No. 102, p. 7 seq.; for the title "land of Canaan" as applied to the Phoenician coast cf. S. A. B. Mercer, *The Tell El-Amarna Tablets* (1939), I, p. 26.
8. E. Sellin and C. Watzinger, *Jericho* (1913).
9. J. Garstang, *Annals of Archaeology and Anthropology, University of Liverpool* (1932), XIX, p. 3 seq.; *ibid.* (1933), XX, p. 3 seq.; *id.* (1934), XXI, p. 99 seq.; *id.* (1935), XXII, p. 143 seq.; *id.* (1936), XXIII, p. 67 seq.
10. *PEQ* (1952), LXXXIV, p. 62 seq.; *ibid.* (1953), LXXXV, p. 81 seq.; *id.* (1954) LXXXVI, p. 45 seq.; *id.* (1955), LXXXVII, p. 106 seq.; *id.* (1956), LXXXVIII, p. 67 seq.; *id.* (1957), LXXXIX, p. 101 seq.; K. Kenyon, *Digging up Jericho* (1957); *BA* (1953), XVI, No. 3, p. 46 seq.; *ibid.* (1954), XVII, No. 4, p. 98 seq.
11. J. and J. B. E. Garstang, *The Story of Jericho* (1948), p. 135 seq.; *LAP*, p. 134 f.
12. *WBA*, p. 79
13. *AJA* (1936), XL, p. 158.
14. M. Noth, *PJB* (1938), XXXIV, p. 7 seq., dismisses the account of the destruction of Ai as an aetiological legend which explained the significance of the Hebrew term.
15. The original name may have been Beth-aven.
16. Josh. 8:28.
17. *BASOR* (1934), No. 56, p. 2 seq.
18. *BASOR* (1939), No. 74, pp. 15 ff.; cf. *BA* (1940), III, No. 3, p. 36.

19. *RB* (1937), XLVI, p. 231 seq.
20. Sir Frederick Kenyon (*The Bible and Archaeology*, 1940, p. 190), has pointed out that the transfer of a name from a devastated or abandoned site to a neighbouring location was a common procedure in ancient Palestine.
21. As identified by Albright, *ZAW* (1929), VI, p. 3.
22. For a full description *vide* O. Tufnell, C. H. Inge and L. Harding, *Lachish II* (*Tell Ed Duweir*), *The Fosse Temple* (1940).
23. This corresponds to the prescriptions for Hebrew sacrifice in Lev. 7:32, and attests to the antiquity of the passage. Cf. *AJA* (1941), XLV, p. 634.
24. *BASOR* (1937), No. 68, p. 23 f.; *ibid.* (1939), No. 74, pp. 20 ff.; cf. *BA* (1938), I, No. 4, p. 26.
25. F. Petrie, *Researches in Sinai* (1906), p. 129 seq.
26. *AASOR* (1936), XVII, p. 79.
27. *ZAW* (1929), VI, p. 1 seq.; *AASOR* (1931), XIII, p. 55 seq.; M. G. Kyle, *Excavating Kirjath-Sepher's Ten Cities* (1934).
28. *AASOR* (1936), XVII, p. 79.
29. Josh. 15:58; *WMTS*, p. 77
30. Josh. 11:10 seq.
31. *BA* (1956), XIX, No. 1, p. 2 seq.; *ibid* (1957), XX, No. 2, p. 34 seq.; Y. Yadin *et al. Hazor I* (1958), p. 5 seq.
32. J. Garstang, *Joshua-Judges* (1931), p. 383.
33. Josh. 11:16 seq.; cf. 10:40 ff.
34. For excavations at Beth-shan *vide AJA* (1941), XLV, p. 483 seq.
35. Cf. Josh. 13:1.
36. A. Götze, *Hethiter, Churriter und Assyrer* (1936), p. 27.
37. Gen. 15:20; Exod. 3:8, 17 *et al.*
38. H. Winckler, *Die im Sommer* 1906 *in Kleinasien ausgeführten Ausgrabungen* (1906).

39. *LAP*, p. 167; J. A. Knudtzon, *Die El-Amarna Tafeln* (1901-05), I, No. 41.

40. *TH*, p. 104 f.

41. *TH*, p. 80 f.

42. *TH*, p. 67.

43. *TH*, p. 68 f.

44. *TH*, p. 88

45. For Hittite legal texts *vide* F. Hrozný, *Code hittite provenant de l'Asie Mineure* (1922); J. M. P. Smith, *The Origin and History of Hebrew Law* (1931), p. 246 seq.; E. Neufeld, *The Hittite Laws* (1951); *AB*, p. 369 seq.; *ANET*, p. 188 seq.

46. *TH*, p. 145 and pl. 9.

47. *TH*, p. 151.

48. *TH*, p. 152 seq. The connection between the Hittite royal festival and the Babylonian New Year festival is tenuous at best.

49. *TH*, p. 156 seq.

50. For the earlier reports *vide* C. F. A. Schaeffer, *Syria, Revue d'Art orientale et d'archéologie* (1929), X, p. 285 seq.; *ibid.* (1931), XII, p. 1 seq.; *id.* (1932), XIII, p. 1 seq.; *id.* (1933), XIV, p. 93 seq.; *id.* (1934), XV, p. 105 seq.; *id.* (1935), XVI, p. 141 seq.; *id.* (1936), XVII, p. 105 seq.; *id.* (1937), XVIII, p. 125 seq.; *id.* (1938), XIX, p. 193 seq.; *id.* (1939), XX, p. 277 seq.

51. Cf. *Orientalia* (1950), XIX, p. 374 seq.

52. *ANET*, p. 129 seq.; *ANE*, p. 92 seq.; C. H. Gordon, *Ugaritic Handbook* (1947), p. 129 seq.; *UL*, p. 11 seq.

53. The practice of astrological consultation prior to battle originated in Babylonia, where astrologers were important members of the military forces, and continued to exercise an influence until the Roman period. During the Second World War the United States military authorities appointed Sydney

Omarr to full-time duty as an astrologer while he was serving in Okinawa in 1945. His assignment was to conduct a regular radio programme, answering questions astrologically on every conceivable subject requested by area service and civilian personnel alike. It would appear that the wheel has come almost to full circle.

54. A generic name for deity in north-west Semitic tongues. Cf. Gen.33:20, 46:3; Josh. 22:22.
55. *LAP*, pl. 60.
56. Compare the position of the weather god of Hatti in the Hittite pantheon.
57. *UL*, p. 9 seq.
58. *FSAC*, p. 317 f.
59. *BA* (1945), VIII, No. 2, pp. 55 ff.
60. *UL*, p. 15.
61. Cf. Ps. 68:4, 104:3.
62. Cf. Ps. 2:4, 103:19.
63. Cf. Ps. 18:13, 77:18, 144:6.
64. 1 Sam. 11:1 seq.
65. 1. 165 seq.; *UL*, p. 99.
66. 62. 50; *UL*, p. 49.
67. *ARI*, p. 76; *FSAC*, p. 234; *WBA*, pl. 68.
68. Baal Epic II. 7 seq.; *UL*, p. 17 f.
69. *ARI*, p. 77.
70. Cf. Jer. 2:20.
71. Cf. Lev. 17:6.
72. *ARI*, p. 92.
73. *ARI*, p. 78.
74. Perhaps El or Baal. Sacred pillars were connected with Patriarchal religion (Gen. 28:18 seq., 31:44 seq.) and probably commemorated a theophany or a covenant.
75. *BA* (1950), XIII, No. 2, p. 31 and pl. 6.
76. Thus "altar of incense" must now be accepted as the correct rendering for "sun-image" in Lev.

26:30; 2 Chron. 14:5, 34:4, 7; Isa. 17:8, 27:9; Ezek. 6:4, 6.

77. Cf. 1 Sam. 2:12 seq.

78. Judg. 5:2 seq.

79. Judg. 5:19 ff.

80. *BASOR* (1940), No. 78, p. 8 f.

81. A. Alt, *Die Staatenbildung der Israeliten in Palästina* (1930), p. 31 seq.

82. *FSAC*, p. 283 f.

83. Josh. 22:10 seq.; Judg. 8:1 seq., 20:12 seq.

84. 1 Sam. 8:5. For the manner in which the warning of Samuel characterised contemporary Canaanite kingship *vide BASOR* (1956), No. 143, p. 17 seq.

CHAPTER V

1. R. A. S. Macalister, *The Excavation of Gezer* (1912). 3 Vols.

2. R. A. S. Macalister, *Bible Side-Lights From the Mound of Gezer* (1906), p. 25.

3. *PEQ* (1937), LXIX, p. 67 seq.

4. C. Watzinger, *Denkmäler Palästinas I* (1933), p. 63 f.; *LAP*, pl. 49.

5. *BASOR* (1943), No. 92, p. 16 seq.

6. R. A. Macalister, *A Century of Excavation in Palestine* (1930), p. 69; E. Grant, *Beth Shemesh* (1929); *ibid. Ains Shems Excavations* (1931-39), 5 Vols.

7. 1 Sam. 4:10.

8. *BASOR* (1933), No. 52, p. 6 seq.; *AP*, p. 118 seq.

9. Judg. 19.

10. *AP*, pl. 30; *WMTS*, p. 141 f.

11. Cf. *AASOR* (1924), IV, p. 51 f.; *WBA*, p. 122.

12. 1 Sam. 13:19 seq.; *AJA* (1939), XLIII, p. 458 seq.;

JBL (1941), LX, p. 36 f. The chief opponents of the prophet Samuel have emerged in much clearer perspective as a result of excavations in the vicinity of Gezer.

13. *LAP*, p. 83.

14. *ARI*, pp. 125 ff.

15. C. H. Gordon, *Ugaritic Handbook* (1955), p. 272, No. 1934; cf. No. 1991.

16. 1 Kings 4:31; 1 Chron. 2:6.

17. The Hebrew *maḥōl* is similar in meaning to the Greek "orchēstra", a semi-circular area in which the Greek chorus danced.

18. The Hebrew *Ezrah* in 1 Kgs. 4:31, 1 Chron. 2:6, means "aboriginal".

19. *WBA*, p. 94.

20. The different sources underlying the account of David's introduction to Saul produce curious results (2 Sam. 21:19; 1 Chron. 20:5). The Mari letters *c.* 1700 B.C. used *davidum* as a title, "chieftain", and consequently it has been suggested that Elhanan was the original name of David.

21. Unfortunately nothing can be assigned with certainty to the Davidic period.

22. F. Kenyon, *The Bible and Archaeology* (1940), p. 176. Similar tunnels were found at Gezer, Megiddo and Gibeon. Cf. R. A. S. Macalister, *The Excavation of Gezer* (1912), I, pp. 256 ff.; R. S. Lamon, *The Megiddo Water System* (1935).

23. Isa. 22:11.

24. *OTC*, p. 149.

25. *ARI*, p. 130 f.

26. R. de Vaux, *RB* (1939), XLVIII, p. 394 seq.; J. Begrich, *ZAW* (1940-41), XVII, p. 1 seq.

27. *AP*, p. 123 seq.

28. 1 Kgs. 4:7 seq.; Cf. W. F. Albright in *Journal of the Palestine Oriental Society* (1925), V, p. 17 seq.; *WBA*, p. 130.

29. *ARI*, p. 132 f.

30. F. Thieberger, *King Solomon* (1947), pp. 150, 275 f.

31. 1 Kgs. 10:28 f. *Qwh*, the Assyrian *Kue*, was Cilicia, famous for its fine horses (Herod. III 90). Cf. *ARI*, p. 135.

32. *ARI*, p. 134.

33. *OTC*, p. 150.

34. *BASOR* (1941), No. 83, p. 21. One inscription from Nora listed the name Tarshish immediately before that of Sardinia, indicating that the Phoenician name of Nora was Tarshish or "Refinery".

35. Phoenician vessels designed for transporting ore and metal were known as "Tarshish ships". F. Thieberger, *King Solomon*, p. 206.

36. Cf. Deut. 8:9. A.V., R.V. "brass" should read "copper".

37. N. Glueck, *The Other Side of the Jordan*, p. 89 seq.

38. 1 Kgs. 7:46.

39. J. A. Montgomery, *Arabia and the Bible* (1934), p. 180.

40. Cf. *BA* (1958), XXI, No. 4, p. 103 f.

41. Cf. Ezek. 40:6 seq.; *BA* (1960), XXIII, No. 1, p. 62 seq.

42. *WBA*, pl. 85. J. W. Crowfoot in *PEQ* (1940), LXXIII, p. 143 seq., attributed the stables to Ahab, but Albright, *AJA* (1940), CLIV, p. 546 seq. dated Stratum IV in the Solomonic period. Cf. *BA* (1941), IV, No. 1, p. 12 f.

43. *AP*, pp. 125 ff.

44. 2 Sam. 5:9; *LAP*, p. 150.

45. *BA* (1941), IV, No. 2, p. 17 seq.; *ibid.* (1944), VII, No. 4, p. 73 seq.; *id.* (1951), XIV, No. 1 p. 8 seq.

46. 1 Kgs. 6:2 seq. The vision of Ezekiel (41:1 seq.) contains detailed measurements agreeing with and

supplementing the account in Kings. Cf. *BASOR* (1950), No. 117, p. 13 seq.

47. *WBA*, pl. 91.

48. *OTC*, p. 148; *ARI*, p. 216 n 65.

49. The foundation ("bosom of the earth") and the top ("the mountain of God") in Ezek. 43:14 ff. are actually Babylonian terms for the base and summit of the *ziggurat*. Cf. *ARI*, pp. 150 ff.

50. Jachin and Boaz, 1 Kgs. 7:21.

51. W. R. Smith, *Lectures on the Religion of the Semites* (1894), p. 487 seq.; *ARI*, p. 144 seq.; *BASOR* (1942), No. 85, p. 18 seq.; *ibid.* (1942), No. 88, p. 19 seq.

52. 1 Kgs. 7:41; cf. Zech. 4:3.

53. The description in Ezek. 43:13 seq. is reminiscent of a *ziggurat*.

54. 2 Chron. 4:6. Cf. *BA* (1949), XII, No. 4, p. 86 seq.

55. *ARI*, p. 148 f.

56. *WBA*, p. 140.

57. *FSAC*, p. 299. Cf. *WBA*, pl. 97.

58. Compare with this the cult of the Apis-bull at Memphis.

59. 2 Kgs. 13:6.

60. 1 Kgs. 12:31.

61. Albright's chronology, *BASOR* (1953), No. 130, p. 4 seq.; *ibid.* (1956), No. 141, p. 26 f., is incorrect. See E. R. Thiele, *The Mysterious Numbers of the Hebrew Kings* (1951), p. 244 seq.; *VT* (1954), IV, pp. 188. ff.

62. M. Noth, *Zeitschrift des Deutschen Palästina-Vereins* (1938), XLI, p. 227 seq.; *VT*, Supp. Vol. IV, (1957), p. 57 seq.

63. *AASOR* (1943), XXI-XXII, p. 29 n 10.

64. *WBA*, pl. 99. The identification of Tell en-Nasbeh with Mizpah is precarious.

65. *BASOR* (1942), No. 87, p. 23 seq.; *ibid.* (1943), No. 90, p. 30 seq.

66. 1 Kgs. 15:18. Cf. *BASOR* (1942), No. 87, p. 26.

67. 1 Kgs. 15:18 ff.

68. 1 Kgs. 20:34. Cf. 1 Kgs. 15:20.

69. 2 Kgs. 8:15.

70. *ANET*, p. 501.

71. *BASOR* (1942), No. 87, p. 14 seq.

72. *BHI*, p. 221.

73. Cf. E. R. Thiele, *The Mysterious Numbers of the Hebrew Kings*, p. 254 seq.

74. 1 Kgs. 16:23 seq.

75. G. A. Reisner, C. S. Fisher and D. G. Lyon, *Harvard Excavations at Samaria* 1908-1910 (1924). 2 Vols. These archaeologists pioneered the stratigraphic method of excavation.

76. J. W. Crowfoot, K. M. Kenyon and E. L. Sukenik, *The Buildings at Samaria* (1942).

77. *WBA*, pl. 101, 104.

78. 1 Kgs. 22:38.

79. *WBA*, pl. 103; J. W. and G. M. Crowfoot, *Early Ivories from Samaria* (1938); J. W. Crowfoot *et al.*, *Objects From Samaria* (1957); A Parrot, *Samaria, The Capital of the Kingdom of Israel* (1958).

80. Cf. Amos 6:4.

81. Amos 3:15; 1 Kgs. 22:39, *et al*

82. W. H. Bennett, *Hastings's Dictionary of the Bible* (1911), III, p. 407; *LAP*, p. 157 and pl. 67. Cf. C. S. Clermont-Ganneau, *La Stèle de Mésa* (1887); *ANET*, p. 320 f.

83. *ARAB*, I, Sect. 590, 816. The expression "Jehu of Beth-Omri" (*Bit-Humri*) is equivalent to "Jehu of Israel", following the custom of naming a kingdom after its founder. Cf. B. Landsberger, *Sam'al I* (1948), p. 19.

84. *ARAB*, I, Sect. 443.

85. *ARAB*, I, Sect. 611.
86. A. H. Layard, *Nineveh and its Remains* (1849), I, p. 282; cf. C. J. Gadd, *The Stones of Assyria* (1936), p. 48.
87. *LAP*, p. 173 and pl. 73; *ANET*, p. 281.
88. An inscription of Shalmaneser III from Assur stated that "Hazael, son of a nobody, seized the throne". *WMTS*, p. 281.
89. Two parallel walls joined together by cross-walls, the outer one almost six feet thick and the inner one about three feet thick.
90. Traces of a red line on the stones proved to be the marks used for vertical and horizontal adjustment of the various courses.
91. 2 Kgs. 6:24 seq.
92. 2 Kgs. 17:5.
93. *WBA*, pl. 110 (*a*).
94. For a suggestion that the seal dates to Jeroboam I *vide* S. Yeivin, *JNES* (1960), XIX, p. 205 seq.
95. *AB*, p. 456; A. T. Olmstead, *History of Palestine and Syria* (1931), p. 420.
96. *UC*, p. 36 seq.
97. As Gen. 38:18 indicates, they were in use at a much earlier period amongst the Hebrews.
98. Cf. J. W. Jack, *Samaria in Ahab's Time* (1929), p. 37 seq.
99. *DOTT*, p. 204 seq.; *ANET*, p. 321.
100. Abiezer, Helek, Shechem, Shemida, Noah and Hoglah.
101. Num. 26:30 seq.; Josh. 17:2.
102. Cf. *WBA*, p. 158.
103. Amos 6:6. For the historical background of the Samaritan ostraca *vide* B. Maisler, *Journal of the Palestine Oriental Society* (1948), XXI, p. 117 seq.

104. 2 Kgs. 15:9.

105. *ARAB*, I, Sect. 816; 1 Kgs. 15:19. Tiglathpileser, known to Israel as Pul, was probably originally named Pulu. Cf. *JNES* (1944), III, p. 156.

106. 2 Kgs. 16:7.

107. *ARAB*, I, Sect. 801 f.; 2 Kgs. 15:29 seq. Stratum III of Megiddo was probably destroyed at this time also.

108. 2 Kgs. 17:3 seq.

109. H. Tadmor, *Journal of Cuneiform Studies* (1958), XII, pp. 22 seq., 77 seq.

110. *ARAB*, II, Sect. 55; *ANET*, p. 284 f.

111. 2 Kgs. 18:14.

112. *ARAB*, II, Sect. 240. The exaggeration is characteristic of ancient Near Eastern annals.

113. 2 Kgs. 20:20; 2 Chron. 32:30.

114. *AB*, p. 475; cf. *LAP*, p. 160.

115. *DOTT*, p. 218 seq.

116. C. C. McGown. *The Ladder of Progress in Palestine* (1943), p. 117. For a short epitaph from *c.* 700 B.C. written in a similar script *vide* N. Avigad, *Israel Exploration Journal* (1953), III, No. 3, p. 137 seq.

117. *WMTS*, p. 43 f. The titles *Tartan*, *Rabshakeh* and *Rabsaris* should be rendered *second in command*, *chief officer* and *chief eunuch*.

118. A. H. Layard, *Discoveries Among the Ruins of Nineveh and Babylon* (1875), p. 126 seq.; *WBA*, pl. 117.

119. 2 Chron. 33:10 seq.

120. *ARAB*, II, Sect. 690. Esarhaddon did in fact rebuild Babylon, which Sennacherib had destroyed. Cf. *ARAB*, II, Sect. 646 f.

121. J. P. Free, *Archaeology and Bible History* (1950), p. 215 f.; I Price, *The Monuments and the Old Testament* (1923), p. 364.

122. *IOTT*, pp. 238 ff.; D. W. B. Robinson, *Josiah's Reform and the Book of the Law* (1951). The view

that the document was a forgery foisted upon a credulous king shows a complete lack of understanding of the nature and function of ancient Near Eastern legal codes.

123. *WMTS*, p. 252; cf. *JNES* (1951), X, pp. 128 ff.

124. 2 Kgs. 24:1. For the Aramaic papyrus letter of a neighbouring king who did not submit so quickly *vide BA* (1949), XII, No. 2, p. 46 seq. This letter was probably sent from Ashkelon just before the battle of 601 B.C., in which Nebuchadnezzar was defeated. Cf. *CCK*, p. 29 f.

125. Jer. 22:18.

126. *CCK*, p. 32 seq.

127. *CCK*, p. 25.

128. *CCK*, p. 29.

129. Jer. 52:28 f.; 2 Kgs. 24:12, 25:8. The apparent discrepancy most probably results from the use of a somewhat different system of computation than that obtaining in Babylon. Cf. *BA* (1956), XIX, No. 3, pp. 56 ff.

130. H. Torczyner, *Lachish I, The Lachish Letters* (1938); cf. *BASOR* (1938), No. 70, p. 11 seq.; *ibid.* (1939), No. 73, p. 16 seq.

131. *BASOR* (1940), No. 80, p. 11 seq.; *ibid.* (1941), No. 82, p. 24.

132. For the violence of the destruction *vide* O. Tufnell, *Lachish III, The Iron Age* (1953), p. 57.

133. *DOTT*, p. 212 f.; *ANET*, p. 322.

134. *ANET*, p. 322, *DOTT*, p. 216.

135. Jer. 34:7.

136. *ANET*, p. 322; *DOTT*, p. 214 f.; *BASOR* (1941), No. 82, p. 20 f.

137. *PEQ* (1938), LXX, p. 165 seq.

138. C. H. Gordon, *The Living Past* (1941), p. 189.

139. Jer. 26:20 seq. Torczyner thought that Ostracon V had been addressed to the prophet, but that the

debacle of 598 B.C. had prevented it from being delivered. Cf. H. Torczyner, *The Lachish Letters*, p. 62. For a review of the problem *vide* D. W. Thomas, *The Prophet in the Lachish Ostraca* (1946), p. 7 seq.; *PEQ* (1950), LXXXII, p. 1 seq.; J. Hempel and L. Rost (Ed.), *Von Ugarit nach Qumran* (1958), p. 244 seq.

140. *ANET*, p. 322.
141. Jer. 38:4.
142. *BA* (1938), I, No. 4, p. 30.

CHAPTER VI

1. R. Koldewey, *Das Wieder Erstehende Babylon* (1925), pp. 90 ff.
2. *ANET*, p. 308; *ANE*, p. 205; *DOTT*, pp. 84 ff.
3. *BA* (1942), V, No. 4, p. 49 f.
4. 2 Kgs. 25:27 seq.
5. *DOTT*, p. 224.
6. *WBA*, pl. 125.
7. *JBL* (1932), LI, p. 77 seq.; H. G. May, *American Journal of Semitic Languages and Literatures* (1939), LVI, p. 146 seq.
8. Probably ancient Mizpah. *DOTT*, p. 222.
9. *WBA*, pl. 126.
10. 2 Kgs. 25:23; Jer. 40:8. "Jezaniah" (Jer. 42:1) and Azariah (Jer. 43:2) may also be the same person.
11. *WBA*, pl. 128; *DOTT*, p. 223 f.
12. 2 Kgs. 25:22 seq.; Jer. 40:7. The title of chief steward is a familiar Old Testament term. Cf. 1 Kgs. 4:6, 2 Kgs. 18:18 *et al.*
13. The Ahikam of 2 Kgs. 22:12; Jer. 26:24.
14. The Shaphan of 2 Kgs. 22:3 seq.
15. G. A. Cooke, *The Book of Ezekiel* (1936), p. 4. This is the Khabar canal (there is no separate Babylonian word for "river") of Ezekiel 1:3.

16. Ezek. 3:15.
17. G. A. Cooke, *The Book of Ezekiel*, p. 42. For evidence that Jews were living in this general area between 500 and 400 B.C. *vide* A. T. Olmstead, *History of the Persian Empire* (1948), pp. 299, 356 seq.
18. A. Parrot, *Babylon and the Old Testament* (1958), p. 68 seq.
19. R. Koldewey, *Das Wieder Erstehende Babylon* (1925); *ibid. Das Ischar-Tor in Babylon* (1918).
20. Dan. 4:30.
21. G. Unger, *Babylon. Die heilige Stadt nach der Beschreibung der Babylonier* (1931), p. 59 seq. and pl. 7.
22. A. Parrot, *Babylon and the Old Testament*, p. 26 seq.
23. I. 181.
24. A. Parrot, *Babylon and the Old Testament*, p. 40 seq.
25. W. H. Lane, *Babylonian Problems* (1923), p. 181.
26. Jer. 29:1 seq.
27. Cf. Ezek. 20:1 seq.
28. Cf. Ezek. 20:20.
29. Ezek. 1:2, 8:1, 20:1, *et al.* His vision of abominations in chapter eight belongs to 592 B.C., the date of one of the tablets which mentions "Yaukin, king of the land of Yahud".
30. *UC*, p. 153.
31. *UC*, p. 156 f.
32. *LAP*, p. 190.
33. Dan. 5:30. Thus Daniel would actually be "third" (*i.e.* "a prominent officer of state") in the kingdom.
34. Dan. 5:18.
35. R. P. Dougherty, *Nabonidus and Belshazzar* (1929), pp. 59 ff., 194.
36. *JBL* (1949), LVIII, p. 375.
37. Dan. 6:29.
38. *DOTT*, p. 83.
39. J. C. Whitcomb, *Darius the Mede* (1959), p. 5 seq.
40. *Cyropaedia*, IV 6, VII 5, 26 seq. The translation of Sidney Smith, *Babylonian Historical Texts Relating*

to the Capture and Downfall of Babylon (1924), p. 121, distinguished between Ugbaru and Gubaru.

41. R. A. Parker and W. H. Dubberstein, *Babylonian Chronology 626 B.C.-A.D.45* (1942), p. 11. Cyrus is said to have diverted the course of the Euphrates so as to allow his soldiers to enter the city along the river-bed.

42. Isa. 44:28, 45:1. However, the name Cyrus may be an insertion by a later hand in the form of an explanatory gloss.

43. Political and economic, as well as humanitarian considerations were in view when this edict was promulgated.

44. R. W. Rogers, *Cuneiform Parallels to the Old Testament* (1912), p. 383.

45. Ezra 1:2 seq.

46. Ezra 6:3 ff.

47. E.g., W. O. E. Oesterley and T. H. Robinson, *A History of Israel* (1932), II, pp. 75, 81.

48. Against a polytheistic background Cyrus treated Marduk and the God of Israel as virtually equal.

49. For recent studies cf. *JBL* (1946), LXV, p. 249 seq.; *The Interpreter's Bible* (1954), III, pp. 570 seq., 613 seq.

50. The phrase, "he is the God who is in Jerusalem" (Ezra 1:3) is typical of a polytheistic environment.

51. Ezra 6:2.

52. Ezra 1:11. It may have meant, "O sun god, protect the father". He is probably the Shenazzar of 1 Chron. 3:18. Cf. *JBL* (1921), XL, pp. 108 ff.; *BASOR* (1941), No. 82, p. 16 f.

53. Ezra 2:2, from a common Babylonian form meaning "Offspring of Babylon".

54. Haggai 2:20 seq. Cf. *TJ*, I, p. 50.

55. *BASOR* (1948), No. 109, p. 21 f.

56. Cf. *Journal of the Palestine Oriental Society* (1934), XIV, p. 178 seq.; *BASOR* (1934), No. 53, pp. 20 ff.

57. 1 Chron. 29:7. Cf. Ezra 2:68, 8:27; Neh. 7:70 ff.
58. Cf. R. H. Pfeiffer, *Introduction to the Old Testament* (1941), pp. 812 f., 830, where the theory is advanced that Ezra, Nehemiah and Chronicles were the work of a "Chronicler" who did not live until *c.* 250 B.C.
59. For a comprehensive list of references relating to this matter *vide* H. H. Rowley, *The Servant of the Lord and Other Essays* (1952), p. 131 seq., reprinted from *Ignace Goldhizer Memorial Volume* (1948), Part I, p. 117 seq.
60. E.g., *BHI*, p. 375 seq.
61. *BHI*, p. 377. For an able presentation of the traditional view *vide* J. S. Wright, *The Date of Ezra's Coming to Jerusalem* (1958), p. 5 seq.
62. Cf. A. T. Olmstead, *History of the Persian Empire* (1958), p. 306.
63. Ezra 4:7 seq.
64. Ezra 4:17 seq.; Neh. 1:3.
65. *BHI*, p. 378.
66. *IOTT*, p. 270 n.
67. Cf. Neh. 2:19 f., 4:1 seq.
68. *ANET*, p. 492; *ANE*, p. 281; *DOTT*, p. 264.
69. *JNES* (1956), XV, p. 1 seq. Geshem is known as Gashmu in Neh. 6:6.
70. *The Interpreter's Bible* (1954), III, p. 681 f.
71. *AP*, p. 143 f.
72. *OTC*, p. 154; *BA* (1955), XVIII, No. 2, p. 46 f.
73. *WMTS*, pp. 83, 133; *AP*, p. 149. Whether the name is that of Tobiah who lived in the time of Nehemiah, or one of his descendants, is still uncertain.
74. *WMTS*, p. 111.
75. Ezra 4:7 seq.
76. *ANET*, pp. 222 f., 491 ff.; *ANE*, p. 278 seq.; *DOTT*, p. 256 seq.; E. Sachau, *Aramaeische Papyrus und Ostraka aus einer juedischen Militaer-Kolonie zu Elephantine* (1911), 2 Vols.; A. Ungnad, *Aramäische Papyrus aus Elephantine* (1911); A. Cowley, *Aramaic*

Papyri of the Fifth Century B.C. (1923). Another group of papyri came to light in the Brooklyn Museum in 1947, and were published by E. G. Kraeling under the title, *The Brooklyn Museum Aramaic Papyri* (1953); Cf. *BA* (1953), XV, No. 3, p. 50 seq.

77. It is similar to the procedure adopted by Jeremiah (32:8 ff.).

78. Cf. the large number of Hebrew names in texts recovered from the fifth century B.C. levels at Nippur, *WBA*, p. 206.

79. *LAP*, p. 201 f.

80. An Aramaic letter from king Adon of Askalon to pharaoh Necho of Egypt (*c.* 600 B.C.) shows the extent to which Aramaic had become the *lingua franca* of Palestine before the Babylonian conquest (2 Kgs. 18:26). Cf. *Semitica* (1948), I, p. 43 seq.; *BA* (1949), XII, No. 2, p. 46 seq.

81. *OTC*, p. 154.

82. E.g., A. Bentzen, *Introduction to the Old Testament* (1925), II, p. 192.

83. I. Price, *The Monuments and the Old Testament* (1925), p. 403.

84. Esther 1:2.

85. A. U. Pope (Ed.), *A Survey of Persian Art* (1938), I, p. 351.

86. M. F. Unger, *Archaeology of the Old Testament* (1954), p. 309. Attestable Greek influence in the Near East is considerably earlier than 332 B.C. (*BHI*, p. 395), as evidenced by mid-seventh century B.C. Greek colonies in Egypt at Naucratis and Tahpanes, and the presence of Greek mercenaries in the Egyptian and Babylonian armies at Carchemish in 605 B.C.

88. *AP*, p. 153.

89. *BASOR* (1957), No. 148, p. 27.

90. *BA* (1955), XVIII, No. 4, p. 84.

91. *BA* (1956), XIX, No. 2, p. 26 seq.

CHAPTER VII

1. There are different accounts of the way in which the scrolls were discovered. Cf. *BDSS*, p. 4. For a more detailed recent survey of the discoveries at Qumran and the first decade of study *vide* R. K. Harrison, *The Dead Sea Scrolls*. Teach Yourself Series (1961).

2. *BDSS*, pp. 6 ff.; E. Wilson, *The Scrolls from the Dead Sea* (1955), p. 11 f.

3. Extracts from the Isaiah, War and Hymn scrolls were published in *Megilloth Genuzoth* I and II (1948-50), and the complete text in *Osar ham-Megilloth hag-Genuzoth she-bidhe ha-Unibhersitah ha-'Ibhrith* (1954).

4. A rare Hebrew fragment containing the Ten Commandments and the Shema (Deut. 6:4 ff.), and dated by Albright in the first century B.C. Other scholars have dated it as late as the second century A.D. Cf. G. Margoliouth, *Jewish Encyclopedia* (1904), VIII, pp. 304b, 312b.; N. Peters, *Die älteste Abschrift der zehn Gebote, der Papyrus Nash* (1905); *JBL* (1937), LVI, p. 145 seq.; *BASOR* (1949), No. 113, p. 19; *ibid.* (1949), No. 115, p. 10 seq.; E. L. Sukenik, *Megilloth Genuzoth* (1948), I, p. 14; *JQR* (1949-50), XL, p. 31.

5. Received in Jerusalem March, 15th, 1948.

6. *BA* (1948), XI, No. 2, pp. 21 ff.

7. M. Burrows (Ed.), *The Dead Sea Scrolls of St. Mark's Monastery* (1950-51). Vol. I, *The Isaiah Manuscript and the Habakkuk Commentary*; Vol. II, Fasc. 2, *Plates and Transcription of the Manual of Discipline*.

8. Cf. *BASOR* (1949), No. 115, pp. 8 ff.; *BA* (1956), XIX, No. 1, pp. 22 ff.

9. N. Avigad and Y. Yadin, *A Genesis Apocryphon* (1956).

10. *ADSS*, p. 26.

11. Cf. *BA* (1954), XVII, No. 1, p. 9 f.

12. The letters were addressed to partisans commanded by ben Galgola, who had been attacking the occupying Roman forces *c.* A.D. 132. Cf. *RB* (1953), LX, p. 276 seq.; *ibid.* (1954), LXI, p. 191 f.; *PEQ* (1954), LXXXVI, p. 23 seq. For additional papyrus Bar-Kokhba letters from another Dead Sea cave cf. Y. Yadin, *BA* (1961), XXIV, No. 2, p. 34 seq.; *ibid.* (1961), XXIV, No. 3, p. 85 seq.

13. *BA* (1954), XVII, No. 1, p. 7.

14. *ADSS*, p. 181 seq.

15. J. M. Allegro, *The Treasure of the Copper Scroll* (1960), p. 33 seq.

16. F. de Saulcy, *Voyage autour de la Mer morte* (1853), II, p. 165 f.; F. Clermont-Ganneau, *Archaeological Researches in Palestine* (1896), II, p. 14 f.; G. Dalman, *PJB* (1914), X, p. 10; *ibid.* (1920), XVI, p. 40.

17. Recorded by Josephus, *The Antiquities of the Jews* (1829 ed.), XV, 5, 2, in 31 B.C.

18. For a plan of the community centre *vide The National Geographic Magazine* (1958), CXIV, No. 6, p. 790 f.

19. *ADSS*, p. 88 f.

20. Cf. *ADSS*, p. 90.

21. *RB* (1954), LXI, p. 230 f.; *ADSS*, p. 84 f.

22. Cf. *VDJD*, p. 17.

23. *RB* (1953), LX, p. 103.

24. For an explanation of these designations cf. R. K. Harrison, *The Dead Sea Scrolls*, p. 29.

25. Cf. *BASOR* (1952), No. 125, p. 6; *JQR* (1949-50), XL, p. 370 n.

26. Jer. 32:14.

27. *The Assumption of Moses*, I. 18; *APOT*, II, p. 415.

28. P. Wernberg-Moeller, *The Manual of Discipline* (Stud. Text Des. Jud. I, 1957), p. 4 seq.; *BASOR* (1949), No. 113, pp. 6 ff.; S. A. Birnbaum, *The Qumran (Dead Sea) Scrolls and Palaeography* (*BASOR* Supp. Stud. 13-14, 1952), p. 10 seq.

29. *DJD*, I, p. 39. As H. J. Plenderleith indicated (*Journal of the Transactions of the Victoria Institute* (1950), LXXXII, p. 146 f.), metallic and non-metallic inks could have been used contemporaneously for a long period. Cf. S. A. Birnbaum, *VT* (1951), I, p. 97 f.

30. G. R. Driver in *The Times*, Aug. 23rd, 30th, Sept. 22nd, 1949; R. Eisler, *ibid.* Sept. 8th, 1949; J. Leveen, *id.* Aug. 26th, Sept. 5th, 1949. Cf. M. Wallenstein, *The Manchester Guardian*, Jan. 8th, July 1st, 1949.

31. G. R. Driver, *The Hebrew Scrolls from the Neighbourhood of Jericho and the Dead Sea* (1951), p. 30 seq. Whilst Driver did not exclude an early date for the scrolls, his contentions were challenged immediately by S. A. Birnbaum in *BASOR* (1949), No. 113, pp. 33 ff.; *ibid.* (1949), No. 115 pp. 20 ff.; *PEQ* (1949), LXXXI, p. 140 seq.; *JBL* (1949), LXVIII, p. 161 seq. In 1957 Driver modified his position, reducing his original dating by several centuries.

32. *JQR* (1948-49), XXXIX, pp. 171 seq. 235 seq., 337 seq., *ibid.* (1949-50), XL. pp. 57 seq., 291 seq., 373 seq.; *The Crozer Quarterly* (1950), XXVI, p. 35 seq.; *JQR* (1950-51), XLI, pp. 1 seq., 71 seq., 247 seq.; *ibid.* (1951-52), XLII, p. 133 seq.; *id.* (1952-53), XLIII, pp. 72 seq., 140 seq.; *id.* (1953-54), XLIV, p. 85 seq.; *id.* (1954-55), XLV, pp. 1 seq., 83 seq., 174 seq.; *id.* (1955-56), XLVI, pp. 1 seq., 116 seq.; *id.* (1956-57), XLVII, p. 745 seq.; *id.* (1957-58), XLVIII, pp. 71 seq., 243 seq.; *id.* (1958-59), XLIX, pp. 1 seq., 221 seq.; *id.* (1960-61), LI, pp. 156 seq., 265 seq. Persistent rumours that Dr. Zeitlin has abandoned his militant position on the scrolls are unfounded, for in private correspondence with the author he has reaffirmed his stand that the documents are medieval, and that they have no value either for the Old or New Testaments.

33. For a date *c.* 64 B.C. cf. *VDJD*, p. 84.

34. *BASOR* (1951), No. 123, pp. 24 ff.; *BA* (1951), XIV, No. 1, p. 29.
35. *BASOR* (1950), No. 118, p. 6.
36. *BASOR* (1949), No. 113, p. 23.
37. *BASOR* (1949), No. 115, p. 22.
38. *Megilloth Genuzoth*, I, p. 14 f.
39. 1*QS*, I: 1-15.
40. I: 16-II:18.
41. II: 19-25.
42. II:25, III:12.
43. V:1-IX:26.
44. M. Mansoor, *The Thanksgiving Hymns* (Stud. Text. Des. Jud. III, 1961), p. 33 seq.
45. *DSSHU*, pl. 39, V:5 f.
46. *BA* (1951), XIV, No. 3, p. 60.
47. More properly "right teacher" or "orthodox teacher", but commonly referred to as the "teacher of righteousness".
48. 1QpHab. VII: 3 ff.
49. 1QpHab. X: 4 f. For a survey of the problems connected with his identification cf. *BDSS*, p. 172 seq.
50. Cf. Isa. 23:1; Jer. 2:10; Ezek. 27:6. "Ships of Kittim," presumably a Mediterranean reference, are mentioned in Num. 24:25, Dan. 11:30.
51. *Megilloth Genuzoth*, I, p. 18.
52. E.g., B. Reike, *Studia Theologica* (1949), II, fasc. I, p. 45 seq.; G. Lambert, *Nouvelle Revue Théologique* (1952), LXXIV, p. 259 seq.; H. H. Rowley, *ZFDSS*, p. 62 seq.; A Michel, *Le Maître de Justice d'après les documents de la Mer Morte* (1954), p. 232 seq.
53. R. de Vaux, *RB* (1950), LVII, p. 428 f.; *ibid.* (1951), LVIII, p. 442 f.; M. Delcor, *Les Manuscrits de la Mer Morte: Essai sur le Midrash d'Habacuc* (1951), p. 56 seq.; *ibid. Revue de l'Histoire des Religions* (1952), CXLII, p. 129 seq.
54. J. van der Ploeg, *Bibliotheca Orientalis* (1951), VIII, p. 9

f.; M. H. Segal, *JBL* (1951), LXX, p. 131 seq.;
D. Barthélemy, *RB* (1952), LIX, p. 207 seq.

55. A. Dupont-Sommer, *Revue de l'Histoire des Religions*
(1950), CXXXVII, p. 129 seq.; K. Elliger, *Studien
zum Habakuk-Kommentar vom Toten Meer* (1953),
p. 226 seq.; F. F. Bruce, *Second Thoughts on the
Dead Sea Scrolls* (1956), pp. 72 ff., 138.

56. J. L. Teicher, *Journal of Jewish Studies* (1951), II,
p. 67 seq.; *ibid.* (1952), III, p. 53 seq.; R. Tournay,
RB (1949), LVI, p. 204 seq.; G. Vermès, *Ephemerides
Theologicae Lovanienses* (1951), XXVII, p. 70 seq.
Cf. *Cahiers Sioniens* (1953), p. 3 seq.

57. P. R. Weis, *JQR* (1950-51), XLI, p. 125 seq.; S.
Zeitlin, *ibid.* (1950-51), XLI, p. 251 seq.

58. 1QpHab. VI: 4 f. Cf. A. Dupont-Sommer, *Revue
de l'Histoire des Religions* (1950), CXXXVIII, p. 159.

59. Cf. *ZFDSS*, p. 73 f.; *PEQ* (1956), LXXXVIII, pp. 102
ff.; *La Nouvelle Clio* (1951-52), III-IV, p. 137 seq.;
Josephus, *Wars of the Jews* (1829 ed.), VI, 6.1.

60. 1QS, IX:11.

61. Cf. *ADSS*, pp. 138 ff.

62. *RB* (1952), LIX, pp. 203 ff.; *ADSS*, p. 115. Translated by T. H. Gaster, *The Dead Sea Scriptures in
English Translation* (1956), p. 307 seq.

63. The term is used of a synagogue storage room
for discarded and dilapidated scrolls. Sukenik's
view that 1Q was a *genizah* has been rejected in
favour of the theory of R. de Vaux, *RB* (1949),
LVI, p. 236, that the cave was a secret library. Cf.
P. Kahle, *VT* (1951), I, p. 38 seq.

64. S. Schechter, (Ed. and transl.), *Documents of Jewish
Sectaries* (1910), 2 Vols. Vol. 1, *Fragments of a
Zadokite Work*. Cf. *APOT*, II, p. 785 seq.; S. Zeitlin,
The Zadokite Fragments (*JQR* Monograph Ser. No. 1,
1952); C. Rabin, *The Zadokite Documents* (1954).

65. Equivalent to *CDC*, V:18-VI:2.

66. *ZFDSS*, p. 3.

67. *BA* (1950), XIII, No. 3, p. 54.

68. T. H. Gaster, *The Dead Sea Scriptures in English Translation* (1956), pp. 4, 101 n 23, suggested that Damascus may be merely symbolical and linked with Amos 5:27. R. North, *PEQ* (1955), LXXXVII, p. 34, thought that the migration was from Jerusalem to Judaea, since Damascus was under Nabataean control after 87 B.C. However, Judaea was also in Nabataean territory at this time.

69. For the etymology of this name cf. K. Cook, *The Fathers of Jesus* (1886), II, p. 48 f.

70. *Hist. Nat.* V. 15.

71. *Every Good Man is Free*, written *c.* 10 A.D.

72. *Hypothetica*, XI.

73. *Wars of the Jews*, II, 8.2.

74. *Antiquities of the Jews*, XVIII, 1.5.

75. *The Refutation of All Heresies*, IX, 13 seq., in *The Ante-Nicene Fathers* (1886), V, p. 134 f.

76. *De Vita Contemplativa* (Loeb Class. Lib. Trans.), IX, p. 113 seq.

77. Cf. L. Nemoy, *Hebrew Union College Annual* (1930), VII, p. 326 seq.

78. Cf. *RB* (1950), LVII, p. 417 seq.

79. G. R. Driver, *The Hebrew Scrolls from the Neighbourhood of Jericho and the Dead Sea* (1951), p. 25 f.

80. *ZFDSS*, p. 24 f.; cf. L. Nemoy, *JQR* (1951-52), XLII, p. 127.

81. O. Cullmann in *Neutestamentliche Studien presented to R. Bultmann* (1954), p. 35 seq.

82. J. L. Teicher, *Journal of Jewish Studies* (1951), II, pp. 67 seq., 115 seq. H. E. del Medico identified the righteous teacher with Menahem ben Judah, the Zealot leader, and in this was followed by C. Roth, *The Historical Background of the Dead Sea Scrolls* (1958), pp. 18 ff.

83. CDC, XIII:27; XIV:1.

84. J. van der Ploeg, *Le Rouleau de la Guerre* (Stud. Text. Des. Jud., II, 1951), p. 13 seq.

85. Cf. C. T. Fritsch, *The Qumran Community* (1956), p. 110; W. H. Brownlee, *The Dead Sea Manual of Discipline* (*BASOR* Suppl. Stud. X-XII, 1951), p. 4; R. Marcus, *JBL* (1954), LXXIII, p. 161; C. Rabin, *Qumran Studies* (Scripta Judaica II, 1957.), pp. 59 f., 69 f.

86. Cf. F. Kenyon, *Our Bible and the Ancient Manuscripts* (1939), p. 48.

87. For a survey of scholarly disenchantment with the Rudolf Kittel text of the Old Testament *vide* H. M. Orlinsky in G. E. Wright (Ed.), *The Bible and the Ancient Near East* (1961), p. 114 seq.

88. Cf. *BASOR* (1954), No. 135, p. 32; *VT* (1957) Suppl. IV, p. 148 seq.; K. Elliger, *Studien zum Habakuk-Kommentar vom Toten Meer* (1953), p. 78 seq.

89. D. Beegle, *BASOR* (1951), No. 123, p. 26 seq. Cf. the earlier comments of Burrows in *JBL* (1949), LXVIII, p. 204 f.

90. For a discussion of the textual variants in 1QISa cf. M. Burrows, *BASOR* (1948), No. 111, p. 16 seq.; *ibid.* (1949), No. 113, p. 24 seq. For 1QISb cf. S. Loewinger, *VT* (1954), IV, p. 155 seq.

91. Cf. *BDSS*, p. 109 seq.

92. *BASOR* (1953), No. 132, p. 8 seq.

93. *ADSS*, p. 57 seq.

94. This is clearly indicated by fragments of the Pentateuch from 4Q. Cf. *BASOR* (1956), No. 141, p. 9 seq.

95. For Greek texts of the Minor Prophets and their bearing upon Septuagint studies cf. *RB* (1953), LX, pp. 18 seq., 85 f.; *ADSS*, p. 178 f.

96. Cf. G. B. Gray, *Isaiah I* in International Critical Commentary (1912), pp. lvi, 332 seq., 397 seq.; C. F. Kent, *The Sermons, Epistles and Apocalypses of Israel's Prophets* (1910), pp. 497 ff.

97. *BA* (1949), XII, No. 2, p. 33.

98. E.g., J. A. Montgomery, *Daniel* in International Critical Commentary (1927), pp. 96 ff.; R. H. Pfeiffer, *Introduction to the Old Testament* (1941), p. 598; A. Weiser, *The Old Testament: Its Formation and Development* (1961), p. 315.

99. This contention was challenged in an anonymous review of the present writer's *Dead Sea Scrolls* (Teach Yourself Series, 1961), in the *Times Literary Supplement* (March 31st, 1961, p. 206) as a "tendentious observation", because the two Daniel fragments were related palaeographically to the Isaiah manuscript, dated *c.* 100 B.C. The reviewer has, of course, overlooked the fact that all the manuscripts from 1Q were copies, not originals, and thus a considerably earlier date is required for the original autographs. Perhaps it will be sufficient to quote Burrows (*BDSS*, p. 109) on this general point, "The Book of Isaiah certainly comes from a time several centuries before the earliest date to which this manuscript can be assigned on any grounds." It is such a tenacious adherence to traditional criticisms of Daniel in the face of other opposing facts that leads to the kind of *faux pas* committed by Bright (*BHI*, p. 418), who dates the apocryphal *additions* (my italics) to Daniel *c.* 170 B.C., while assigning the composition of Daniel proper to 166 B.C. It would be instructive to know precisely how this feat was accomplished.

100. These were: 3:24; 7:1; 14:4, 30; 15:9; 21:8; 23:2; 33:8; 45:2, 8; 49:17, 24; 51:19; 56:12; 60:19. Burrows has admitted that the traditional text should have been retained in some of these instances. Cf. *BDSS*, p. 305.

101. Cf. F. M. Cross, *The Ancient Library of Qumran and Modern Biblical Studies* (1958), p. 124 seq.

102. F. M. Cross, *The Ancient Library of Qumran*, p. 145.

SELECT BIBLIOGRAPHY

(of works not mentioned previously.)

Adams, J. M.	*Ancient Records and the Bible*, 1946.
Alt, A.	*Der Gott der Väter*, 1929.
Baikie, J.	*The Sea Kings of Crete*, 1926.
Beadnell, H. J. L.	*The Wilderness of Sinai*, 1927.
Bruce, F. F.	*Biblical Exegesis in the Qumran Texts*, 1959.
Burrows, M.	*More Light on the Dead Sea Scrolls*, 1958.
Carter, H.	*The Tomb of Tut-ankh-Amen*, 1923-27, 2 Vols.
Ceram, C. W.	*The Secret of the Hittites*, 1956. *Narrow Pass Black Mountain* 1956.,
Childe, V. G.	*Piecing Together the Past. The Interpretation of Archaeological Data*, 1956.
Cornfeld, G.	*Adam to Daniel*, 1961.
Cottrell, L.	*The Bull of Minos*, 1953.
Diringer, D.	*The Alphabet*, 1949.
Driver, G. R.	*Aramaic Documents of the Fifth Century*, 1954. *Canaanite Myths and Legends*, 1956.
Driver, G. R. and Miles, J. C.	*The Assyrian Laws*, 1935.
Dupont-Sommer, A.	*The Jewish Sect of Qumran and the Essenes*, 1956.
Elder, J.	*Archaeology and the Bible*, 1960.
Gardiner, A.	*Egypt of the Pharaohs*, 1961.

Glueck, N.	*The River Jordan*, 1946.
Gray, J.	*The Legacy of Canaan*, 1957.
Gressmann, H.	*The Tower of Babel*, 1928.
Harding, G. L.	*The Antiquities of Jordan*, 1959.
Herzfeld, E.	*Archaeological History of Iran*, 1935.
Hitti, K.	*History of Syria*, 1957.
Hogarth, D. G.	*Kings of the Hittites*, 1926.
Ilton, P.	*Digging in the Holy Land*, 1959.
Kahle, P.	*The Cairo Genizah*, 1947.
Kees, H.	*Ancient Egypt*, 1961.
Kelso, J.	*The Ceramic Vocabulary of the Old Testament*, 1948.
Kenyon, K. M.	*Archaeology in the Holy Land*, 1961.
King, L. W.	*A History of Babylon*, 1919. *A History of Sumer and Akkad*, 1923.
Kramer, S. N.	*From the Tablets of Sumer*, 1956. *History Begins at Sumer*, 1958.
Lact, S. J. de	*Archaeology and Its Problems*, 1957.
Langdon, S.	*The Babylonian Epic of Creation*, 1923.
Lloyd, S.	*Foundations in the Dust*, 1949.
Milik, J. T.	*Ten Years of Discovery in the Wilderness of Judaea*, 1959.
Parrot, A.	*Discovering Buried Worlds*, 1955. *Samaria, the Capital of the Kingdom of Irsael*, 1958. *Nineveh and Babylon*, 1961.
Peters, J. P.	*Bible and Spade*, 1923.
Phillips, W.	*Qataban and Sheba*, 1955.
Ploeg, J. van der	*The Excavations at Qumran*, 1958.
Pritchard, J. B.	*Archaeology and the Old Testament*, 1958.

Reed, W. L. *The Asherah in the Old Testament,* 1949.

Rothenberg, B. *God's Wilderness,* 1961.

Schubert, K. *The Dead Sea Community,* 1959.

Smith, S. *Early History of Assyria,* 1928.

Sutcliffe, E. F. *The Monks of Qumran,* 1960.

Wheeler, M. *Walls of Jericho,* 1956.

Winlock, H. E. *The Rise and Fall of the Middle Kingdom in Thebes,* 1947.

Wiseman, D. J. *Illustrations From Biblical Archaeology,* 1959.

Wiseman, P. J. *New Discoveries in Babylonia About Genesis,* 1953.

Woolley, C. L. *Abraham: Recent Discoveries and Hebrew Origins,* 1936.
Excavations at Ur. A Record of Twelve Years' Work, 1955.

Wright, G. E. *The Old Testament Against its Environment,* 1950.

Wright, G. E. and Freedman, D. N. *The Biblical Archaeologist Reader,* 1961.

INDEX